KINTYRE

KINTYRE
Best of All the Isles

by Alasdair Carmichael

DAVID & CHARLES
NEWTON ABBOT   LONDON
NORTH POMFRET (VT)   VANCOUVER

ISBN 0 7153 6317 4

3 / 2 4 6 4

To Sheena, who lived with it

*DA
880
. K56C37
1974*

Set in 11 on 13pt Baskerville and printed
in Great Britain by Latimer Trend &
Company Ltd Plymouth for David &
Charles (Holdings) Limited South
Devon House Newton Abbot Devon

Published in the United States of
America by David & Charles Inc
North Pomfret Vermont 05053 USA

Published in Canada by Douglas David
& Charles Limited 3645 McKechnie
Drive West Vancouver BC

CONTENTS

NOTE: Just as this book goes to press I should like to note that in common with ferry services throughout the Highlands, those in Kintyre are in a state of revision and, in some cases, withdrawal. While the presently much-rumoured oil developments might, on realisation, be expected to stabilise or increase such services, confirmation should always be sought from the relevant shipping company.

ILLUSTRATIONS

ILLUSTRATIONS

Photographs not acknowledged above are by Alex Coupar AIIP

IN TEXT

Drawings by Ann R. Thomas

8

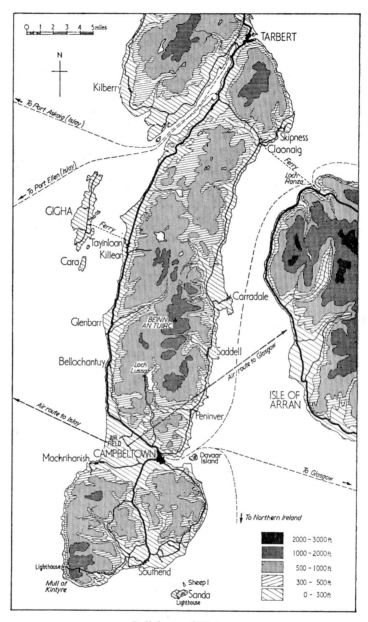

Relief map of Kintyre

1 BEST OF THE ISLES

THE sea-girt coast line of Argyll's mainland is of astonishing extent. He who would walk around it by every inlet and bay, over sand and shingle, boulders and rocks would, at the end of many days, have travelled a distance roughly equal to that from the Clyde to the St Lawrence, an approximate 3,000 miles.

At the most southerly point of his journey, such a walker would find himself clinging to the base of storm-battered cliffs towering for hundreds of vertical feet above him, with contending tides swirling thunderously about his feet, and the green coast of Ireland a bare twelve miles away. He would have reached what the first men to stand on top of those cliffs called *ceann tir*—head of land.

Centuries after the name was first spoken, it was written into early maps and documents as one word: Cantire. By this time the name embraced the whole 300 square miles rolling narrowly northward from those cliffs to a point, 38 road miles to the south of Inveraray town, where, at Tarbert, the glittering waters of Loch Fyne fail by a matter of 1,600 yards to unite with the eager tide of the western ocean that reaches inward from the Sound of Jura.

Between East and West Loch Tarbert, a height of land of approximately 47ft prevents that union of the seas which would make all of the land mass to the south an island in geographical fact, rather than by the somewhat dubious decree of a piratical Norwegian king who successfully claimed its insularity in the year 1098.

Long before that time, and for many centuries after it, the peninsula jutting like a great green pier out from the mainland of Scotland towards Ireland was, geographically, historically and politically perhaps the most contentious area in Scotland. Somewhere along the line the earlier spelling came to be displaced by the anglicised 'Kintyre', the form which is found in most general usage since around the mid-sixteenth century.

LIE OF THE LAND

From the almost negligible isthmus at what the fourteenth-century poet Barbour described as 'betuix the Tarbartis twa', Kintyre thrusts its average 8 mile width southward for around forty variedly fertile miles to the storm-beleaguered Mull, graveyard of many a tall ship. That the spine of the peninsula is formed by much very rough ground is clear from the fact that, after a few miles south of Tarbert, no road crosses it for a full two-thirds of its entire length. This lack of transverse roads is explained by the elevation of the peninsula, which consists of a central spine of hills running almost the entire length, alternating with hollows which form narrow glens carrying fast rushing streams. Nowhere does the chain of hills reach to above 1,500ft, the greatest altitude being attained by Beinn an Tuirc towards the east side, overlooking Carradale Bay, Arran and the Ayrshire coast from 1,491ft.

This very long coastline of the peninsula is, especially on the east side where the land rises more steeply from the sea, indented by numerous small coves and bays, with deep narrow gullies running upward from these into the main spine of hills to where hidden lochs overflow from their hollows. Between those gullies which meet the sea in rounded bays of silver sand, precipitous weather-worn cliffs rise starkly from the tide's edge.

The west side, on the other hand, is of a physical character so completely different that it might easily be taken for another isle or peninsula, and not in the same country. Here, where great broad areas of light but fertile sandy soil intervene between the present sea level and the clearly discernible raised beach of the post-glacial age, the lower slopes of the hills rise much more gently and gradually towards the steeps of the central spine.

GEOLOGY

This sparsely covered central spine, mainly of Quartzose Micaschist, which runs uniformly southward from the isthmus, is interrupted where the sea makes its deepest indentation into the land, at Campbeltown Loch on the east, just opposite to where the bay of Machrihanish makes a lesser inroad from the Atlantic. This, the narrowest part of the peninsula, is a low-lying plain of peat moss about 4½ miles in width, known as the Laggan of Kintyre; once—thousands of years ago—an impassable morass, and later a useful source of peat, this area has of more recent times been reclaimed as extremely productive farmland.

It is fair to conclude that this narrow waist, or *laggan*, once made the mountainous land mass south of here to the Mull a separate isle. In the section dealing with the pre-history of the peninsula it will be noted that traces of the earliest human habitation are confined to the most southerly area; this gives weight to the not unreasonable theory that, even as lately as 6,000 years ago, the sea level had combined with the low mossy Laggan to form a 4 mile wide barrier of water, or, more likely and less passable, a broad trackless area of dangerous fenland.

Smoothed and striated rock surfaces on the higher parts of the peninsula, as well as characteristic deposits, tell their tale of Kintyre's earliest beginnings following on the last ice age, when enormous glaciers or sheets of ice, estimated to have been, in places, 5,000ft in thickness, moved slowly southward over the Scottish Highlands, diverging eastward and west somewhere north of where Inverness now stands, one branch to gouge out the north-western sea lochs towards the Hebrides before the

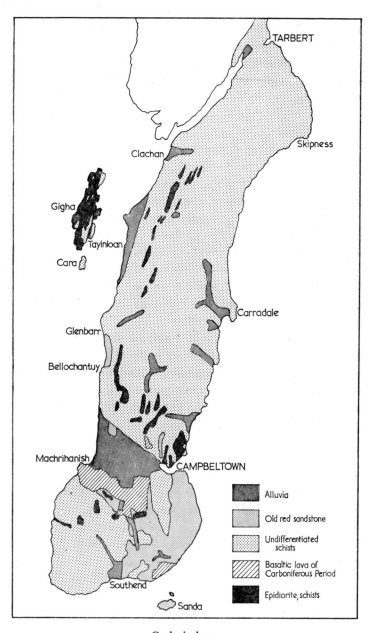

TARBERT

Skipness

Clachan

Gigha

Tayinloan

Cara

Carradale

Glenbarr

Bellochantuy

Machrihanish

CAMPBELTOWN

Southend

Sanda

Alluvia

Old red sandstone

Undifferentiated
schists

Basaltic lava of
Carboniferous Period

Epidiorite, schists

Geological map

other was pressed back towards Britain again by the weight of the even more massive Scandinavian sheet which was moving roughly towards the Yorkshire coast. It was this contention of the two mightily opposing forces which bulldozed out the bed of what became the Clyde valley as well as all the long, deep narrow lochs of Argyll—including, of course, Loch Fyne and Kilbrannan Sound, the West Loch and the Sound of Jura, before pressing on to reach Ireland, Wales and the English Midlands, where, incidentally, boulders of the granite of Ailsa Craig have been found, left there by the passing of the gigantic ice sheet of 10–12,000 years ago.

It was soon after this period that the rising sea from the melting ice caps met at the Straits of Dover, cutting Britain off from an area stretching as far as the Mediterranean, over which earlier human wanderers had been able to move on foot, as they pleased. The same rising ocean level formed what we now call the Irish Sea, and Kintyre was born; not, undoubtedly, a peninsula as later adjustment of the sea level was to leave it; not one isle, but two, separating at the low Laggan between Campbeltown Loch and Machrihanish; and with most of what is now the most fertile land all along the west coast deep under the waves.

From Tarbert south, Quartzose Micaschist predominates in the composition of the peninsula, although a narrow band of Metamorphic Limestone, as well as an adjacent narrower band of those metamorphic rocks collectively known as Green Beds, runs almost the full length. Both to north and south of the town of Campbeltown there are good broad patches of limestone where, as might be expected, the pastureland is particularly lush. Between the town and the village of Southend 10 miles to the south, as well as on coastal strips all down the west side, Old Red Sandstone provides the basis for the notable arable agriculture of the area. Much less common to the West Highlands, however, is the exposure of carboniferous strata running west of the town through to the sea at the village of Machrihanish.

This carboniferous exposure, of which only three other small patches have been noted in Argyll, includes some typical fossiliferous limestone, as well as coal measures both barren and productive. The somewhat up and down story of the mining of this coal over the centuries will be related in another chapter. Large dairy herds thrive today in this particular area where, in former days, much of the barley needed for the distillation of whisky was grown.

The greater part of the coastline, especially on the west, is typical raised beach, giving long narrow strips of that light but rich sandy soil on which the arable economy of the peninsula is largely based. On the west side, both the raised beach and the lower slopes of the hills above are cultivated and excellently productive. On the east side, the hills tend to rise more steeply from closer to the present sea level. The higher spine of the peninsula, though displaying to the distant eye more of green than of purple or brown, is, in the main, bleak, shallow and heath-covered, affording a living only for the hardy breed of black-face sheep long accustomed to thrive on barer hills than these.

Worthy of note, on the east side of the peninsula, 13 miles northward from Campbeltown, is the alluvial strath of Carradale which extends for almost five miles in a northerly direction, and at a full half mile in width. Here, where the slow-moving river loops widely, the excellent arable land is sheltered to both north and east by wooded hills rising fairly steeply to between 700ft and 1,000ft.

CLIMATE

Due to the influence of the warm sea currents of the Gulf Stream, the climate of Kintyre is mild, inclining to moist—a term which mustn't be confused with 'rainy', as will be shown.

Snow is so rare, especially in the more southerly parts of the peninsula, as to be remarkable. Fog is practically unheard of. Temperatures in summer frequently top the 80s F for long

Page 17 (*above*) Tarbert's peaceful landlocked harbour. A colourful fair has been held in this village since the fourteenth century; (*below*) golden sands near Southend. The modern building to the left is the Keil Hotel

Page 18 (*above*) Rock cleft at Tarbert almost filled with emptied scallop shells, the waste from the sea-food factory in the village. This 'shell bay' is a favourite picnic spot with visitors; (*right*) Dunaverty Crag, scene of an important episode in Kintyre's history

periods, only the sea-borne south-westerly winds along the coasts keeping the thermometer a little lower than even slightly inland. Nor is there a sharp drop overnight. Since all of the area south of Ronachan enjoys an average daily four hours of sunshine throughout the year, Kintyre is often, winter or summer, among the few places in the west to report a sunny day when, on the Clyde coast and northward towards Oban also, the report has been of continuous rain.

The prevailing south-westerly winds are, on the average, soft and warm, though these, from November to the end of March, can and frequently do increase to black storm force with little warning, riding on sleet which lowers the temperature with incredible speed, and sends gigantic seas crashing icily on every shore of the peninsula.

The high average of sunshine hours is built up mostly during late May, June and early July, when day often follows warm sunny day, with scarcely a break that is sufficiently dark to be called night, between sunset and sunrise.

The average rainfall over the whole area is around 50in, being as low as 45in for the whole of the west coast arable strip and the adjacent offshore Isle of Gigha, where semi-tropical plants flourish, astonishingly, in the open. Rainfall is naturally somewhat higher away from the coastal strip and over the hills, reaching a maximum of 70in only in the area of Beinn an Tuirc, the highest point on the peninsula. This compares very favourably with the vast bulk of the nearby mainland areas of Argyll, where averages of 80, 90 and 100in are common, due to the very much higher hills.

FLORA

The comparatively recent tree plantings of the Forestry Commission, particularly in the Carradale and Saddell districts, have shown that pine, larch and spruce grow readily and fast, as they do in the west side of Kintyre also, where privately owned forests are of longer establishment. Alder, ash and birch

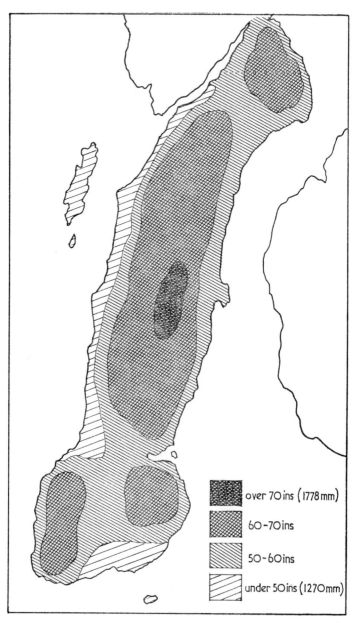

over 70 ins (1778 mm)

60 – 70 ins

50 – 60 ins

under 50 ins (1270 mm)

Rainfall map

thrive where they are found, but these are far from plentifully distributed, which is the case also with beech, elm, poplar, plane and even rowan. Where it occurs along the east side, rowan is to be found ablaze with red berries a full month before such fruit is even tinged with brown in the mainland districts of the county. It is therefore less surprising than it might be to find thriving specimens of the cordyline and cabbage palms, natives of Australia, flourishing extensively, not only in the public and private gardens all along the sea front at Campbeltown, but even on the east side of the Isle of Gigha where the exposure might be expected to be severe and the east wind often hard.

Among the many wild flowers, primroses appear in outstanding profusion, forming a delicately-scented carpet everywhere in spring, to be followed not much later by the colourful mixture of thrift and wild hyacinths. Yellow flag irises wave in large patches surrounded by scented bog myrtle; wild cotton blows and nods in the more marshy areas, where also are to be found a few butterfly orchids, bog asphodel, bog-bean and yellow globe flowers. On some of the hill lochs pure white water lilies are common, and in the vicinity of the lochs the flesh-eating sundew and the little pale butterwort thrive side by side.

Nearer to the sea shore may be seen the beautiful vernal squill (*Scilla maritima,* or sea-onion) with grass of parnassus in the damper spots, and, often among crops, both the large white daisy and its gayer counterpart in brilliant yellow. Queen of the meadow is everywhere. The fleeting, shy wild rose has its own special place, most especially on the great moorland stretch of the one time battlefield of Rhunahaorine, where these tiny red flowers blow in such density that they are still believed by many to have sprung there blushing for the blood that was spilled where now only the soft wind from the sea stirs their blossoms. Woodland edges and all outcrops of rock are covered, late in summer, with several shades of ling and bell heather, ranging from the rare pure white through pink to the deepest purples and reds.

Cultivated plants which would, almost anywhere else in the country, require at least cold greenhouse protection, thrive readily in Kintyre. Naturally these are such as prove themselves impervious to salt-laden winds, or which have somehow developed immunity. Besides the varieties of palm already noted, fuchsias appear everywhere, seeding themselves riotously from hedge to hedge. In the spring and early summer, rhododendrons, especially on Gigha's rocky isle, make a dazzling blaze of colour, aided by azaleas, primulas and camellias. Later, into autumn, hydrangeas, glearias and embothriums take over the colourful stage. It is remarkable to note that, while these and other supposedly tender subjects stand up to the salt-laden winds and indeed thrive in the conditions, other plants, notably holly and laurel, as well as certain reputedly hardy varieties of rhododendron must be given shelter from these winds or their loss is certain.

FAUNA

Among the larger mammals to be found in Kintyre, red deer, recently believed to be on the increase from near extinction in the late 1950s, are at the time of writing once again so hard to find that the species may be discounted. Roe deer find sanctuary in the afforestated areas, and Japanese and Sika deer, of comparatively recent introduction to the east side of the peninsula, have spread to the west and appear to be on the increase.

The brown hare is abundant, the blue or mountain hare less so. Foxes, which had been eradicated and successfully kept out of Kintyre for a full century, have made their appearance since around the close of World War II. Rabbits were plentiful here as elsewhere in the West Highlands till the introduction of myxomatosis; certain remote colonies, however, appear to have escaped the scourge, and though numbers are very much reduced overall, recolonisation must remain a possibility.

Badgers and wild-cats are not readily seen, but are less rare than is often supposed. Otters, too, may be observed by the patient watcher near the mouths of the few rivers. Among the smaller creatures, stoat, weasel, hedgehog, mole, common and water shrew, brown rat, short-tailed and water vole, long-tailed field mouse and pipistrelle bat are of as wide distribution as throughout the mainland area of Argyll.

Reptiles are covered by three species only—the adder, slow-worm and common lizard. Frogs and toads are abundant.

The offshore Isle of Gigha must be separated from the rest of Kintyre in the important field of mammals; not only are there no deer or foxes to be found there, but badgers, hares, stoats, weasels and moles are also absent. Seals are plentiful about the rocky coastline, and otters may be seen, if only occasionally, in the vicinity of nearby Cara Island.

BIRD LIFE

What Gigha may lack in variety of earthbound creatures is more than compensated for in its distribution of bird life. On this sea-indented isle, which measures a rough six miles long by about a mile and a half across, competent observers have noted around seventy different kinds of birds, ranging in size from the tiny wren to both mute and whooper swans.

Here are found not only those birds in general distribution throughout the peninsula, but large colonies of some not readily observed elsewhere. To the south-west the bay of Eun Eilean—Bird Isle—is a veritable sanctuary for eider, fulmar, shelduck and black-throated diver, among others which are more common throughout. Oystercatchers abound, as do terns, mergansers and the occasionally observed scoter petrel.

Garbh Eilean, at the north-west end of the isle and connected to it by a tidal strand, is one vast gullery, loud with the presence of the guillemots and gulls which breed on the rocky ledges in huge numbers. Not surprisingly, peregrine falcons have been observed there also, though these are thought to nest only on nearby Cara. Mallard, wigeon, pochard and teal are all there, though not in large numbers. Ravens and hooded crows nest on Gigha, as elsewhere throughout Kintyre; but of greater interest in the small isle is the growing heronry on what was once a mill loch, stocked with small trout, from which as many as sixteen herons have been counted taking to the air on the one alarm.

Amongst game birds here, as throughout the peninsula, pheasant, grouse and snipe have their place. Partridges are thought to be extinct, since none have been reported for more than twelve years.

On the main peninsula, the hen harrier, a comparatively recent arrival, is now regarded as established. Wood pigeon, curlew and golden plover are also to be seen, though the latter not in such numbers as the humble woodcock which, in winter, comes from less hospitable areas to the kindly green softness of Kintyre.

In this area as elsewhere, constant changes in the habits and movement of birds are to be noted. To take one example, owls and buzzards seem actually to have turned man's inventiveness to their purposes, since these two predators are nowadays most frequently to be seen perched on power lines and telephone poles, waiting for the motor car to do the work of killing which they have apparently realised it is better equipped even than they are to accomplish. Other changes of habit are less easily explained, as in the case of the greylag or white-fronted geese which, up to 1930, never overwintered in Kintyre. Since that year, hundreds pass the winter here; is it possible that, up till then, smaller numbers in the flocks rendered the search for new pastures unnecessary? Or has the emphasis on dairy farming made the winter grass more attractive? Red and black grouse have, on the other hand, become very much scarcer over the same period, a scarcity that cannot be entirely unconnected with the noticeable increase in the numbers of black-backed gulls and buzzards—that increase being itself understandable, since fewer lairds maintain gamekeepers in these days.

Waxwings are occasional and fleeting visitors to Kintyre, but have been noted in quite large flights on the west side. Singing birds are mainly those common to other parts of the county and neighbouring isles; but in very few places can the volume of lark song exceed that which delights any visitor to that glorious waste of machair stretching far beyond the sand dunes above the 3 mile crescent of beach between Westport and Machrihanish.

Incidentally, it has only of recent years been realised that Kintyre must lie on the flight-path for many southward bound migratory flocks. The many unusual species fleetingly observed at Skerryvore lighthouse may well prove easier of study from the broader acres of the peninsula, with a likely valuable increase in such knowledge as is now possessed on the migratory habits of birds.

2   PREHISTORIC KINTYRE

FOR the archaeologist, whether he be a professional bent on uncovering hitherto unsuspected secrets of the distant past, or just the interested wanderer, amazed by how much of a way of life as it was lived many thousands of years back stands revealed in ancient tools, ornaments, utensils, graves and buildings, there is in these islands no field richer than Kintyre.

Throughout the peninsula from Tarbert to the Mull, very many sites of prehistoric human habitation are easy of access. Before visiting any of these, however, it might be well to know what sort of people lived there and what kind of lives they lived. A great deal of what has been learnt about them—for it must be remembered that the earliest written records of Scottish life go no farther back than the departure of the Romans—has been pieced together from the evidence of tools, utensils and ornaments found in their tombs and near the places where they lived. Since a good collection of these is housed in the museum section of Campbeltown Library, a long visit should be made there before any field viewing is undertaken.

It was about the mid-nineteenth century that a wave of interest in the distant past swept over the country. The earliest inhabitants of Britain were named—and dated—from the implements they had used and the materials from which these were made. Hence the Stone, Bronze and Iron Ages were so called, in the order in which such materials had been in use.

Later investigation sub-divided these groups into more exact periods of time, as design and technique were seen to advance, so that each age had its early, middle and late civilisations. These sub-divisions were themselves further broken up into cultures with names like 'Beaker People' and 'Food Vessel People'—the only method by which they can now be identified, since there is no way of knowing what they called themselves, or by what name the successive waves of arrivals became known to the earlier peoples into whose territories they wandered. It must be understood that these ages cannot be tied to any hard and fast date other than in relation to a particular area; for example, in Kintyre, the Mesolithic, or Middle Stone Age, period might well have coincided with the Paleolithic, or Old Stone Age, in, say, Ardnamurchan. Similarly there may be today, perhaps somewhere in New Guinea, a people graduating slowly from Mesolithic to Neolithic, or New Stone Age, as more advanced tribes bring in new methods of farming and hunting.

MESOLITHIC MAN (4000–3000 BC)

In Kintyre, then, the earliest human inhabitants of whom there is so far any evidence appeared about six to seven thousand years ago, that is, at the latest, 4000 BC. These people lived by hunting and fishing, and probably moved about in small groups, never far from the sea coast. The distinctive working of their small flint implements places them in the Mesolithic Period, or Middle Stone Age, that is, around 4000–3000 BC. That these hunters wandered into Kintyre from the south and not by the mainland route from Tarbert seems clear from the fact that some of the flint utensils found are comparable with similar fragments from the Solway area. Also, all the Kintyre flints which have so far come to light have been in the most southerly part of the peninsula, mostly from building excavations around and in Campbeltown itself, at the Calton housing scheme, the Springbank distillery, the Albyn distillery and at Millknowe and Dalaruan—the most distant ones being found at Machrihanish. The large quantities of waste flakes of flint

must indicate an industry in the making of flint implements—
all of which, incidentally, lie just above the level of the 25ft
raised beach.

NEOLITHIC AGE (3000–2000 BC)

Around 3000 BC, the hunters and fishers were joined by the
earliest Kintyre farmers. These Neolithic immigrants still used
stone tools, implements and weapons, but based their economy
much less on hunting than on agriculture. These newcomers
are thought to have arrived in South Kintyre by sea, probably
crossing from nearby Ireland—though there is evidence of
their ancestors having wandered, over a space of hundreds of
years and many generations, through Europe, being possibly
of Levantine origin. They brought with them the first half-wild
seeds of crops, such as wheat, barley and rye, and naturally
chose for their farming the light, gravelly soils which were most
easily cultivated by their primitive hand-cultivators—probably
curved sharpened sticks. They also introduced the first domestic
livestock to Kintyre. Their stone tools, especially the polished
axes, were vastly improved over anything possessed or made
by the Mesolithic hunters.

Over the following thousand or so years, this race of people
established themselves all over the south-west of Scotland, their
areas of habitation easily identified by their characteristic
communal burial cairns—labelled, for identification purposes,
the Clyde-Solway group of cairns. Of the hundred or so
examples of this particular burial cairn so far identified, eleven
are noted in Kintyre—ten of them to the south and east of the
peninsula, where the alluvial deposits of the raised beaches
suited their kind of farming. The single-chambered burial
cairn of this period found in West Kintyre, at Beacharr, is often
regarded as the finest example, and is certainly the largest. It
was excavated first in 1892 and again in 1959 and 1961. In
each of its three compartments were found two round-bottomed
pots of a distinctive type which gave the name Beacharra Ware

to this kind of pottery, wherever it was subsequently discovered. These, along with a belt fastener of jet also from this cairn, may be seen in the Campbeltown Museum.

Those communal graves, probably used over and over again for generations, are formed of massive stone slabs set on edge, forming a chamber averaging 20ft long by about 4ft across. The chamber can in most cases be entered by way of a narrow gap between two big end slabs, which gap was sometimes walled up by dry stone, or protected by a single door slab. The entire structure was then buried in a cairn—a vast, elongated pile of rounded stones, sometimes confined by a sort of boulder kerb around the verges. Only three out of the eleven Neolithic burial cairns found in Kintyre have so far been subjected to excavation.

BRONZE AGE (2000–500 BC)

Around 4,000 years ago, a new race with new implements, weapons and burial customs seems to have arrived in Kintyre. Since they carried with them the first articles of worked metal known in the peninsula—or in Scotland, for that matter—they became the earliest representatives of the Bronze Age. The small daggers of copper or bronze carried by these newcomers were probably few in number. These people were of a different race, however, from the Stone Age settlers—with whom there is evidence of their later integration—being short of stature, thick set and round-headed, and are believed to have wandered, over the centuries, from Eastern Europe.

Their distinctive type of pottery jars gives them the label of Beaker People. The vessels of this type which gave them the name were found in their burial places. These were not the communal chambers of the Stone Age, but characteristic individual stone coffins, or 'cists', in which the dead were placed in a crouched, knees-up posture. Many such cists have been noted in Kintyre, and articles found, including a typical beaker, are on display in the Campbeltown Museum. Most of the cist

29

burials are of one grave to one site, but in a few cases several have been grouped together in the form of a small cemetery. Perhaps the most interesting of these multiple cist sites came to light in 1959 during ploughing in a field of Kilmaho Farm, near Campbeltown. Of the three cists, one showed signs of earlier investigation, the adult bones having been disturbed and scattered. The second contained the undisturbed remains of not one, but two adult bodies, as well as a small flake of flint. The third and best preserved of the group contained the bones of what proved to be an adult of middle age, in the characteristic crouched position and laid on its right side. With the bones a food vessel stood just as it must have been placed, and near to where the dead hands may have grasped them were two flint knives, a small riveted knife of bronze, a bronze awl and several human teeth. These finds are on display in Campbeltown Museum.

This burial is of particular interest in that it bridges three periods, showing that flint knives were treasured as late as, say, 1500 BC when bronze tools were in use, and by which time the culture of the Beaker People was being displaced by that of the Food Vessel People—again named from the distinctive pottery ware found in their burial places.

These Food Vessel Folk, like the Beaker People, buried their dead in stone cists. By now, pins of bone and bronze for fastening clothing were coming into use, as well as ornaments of jet—a very fine necklace of which rare material is preserved in Campbeltown Museum.

It is to be supposed that, already, trade routes were being opened up. These latest arrivals may indeed have been attracted to South Argyll by the rich deposits of copper, which they needed for the increased manufacture of bronze axes and other weapons now coming into use. Probably the newcomers came from Ireland, where in the south, there was a supply of the tin necessary for the hardening of copper into bronze; the next nearest source of tin would have been Cornwall.

From carvings on graves of this period found in the Kilmartin area of the mainland, it would seem that this was the time when those mysterious symbols known as cup marks, or cup and ring marks, first made their appearance. These symbols—in the form of a group of deeply ground hollows, not in every case surrounded by ring-marks of lesser depth—have not, to date, been found on grave slabs or cists in Kintyre, as they have been in Mid Argyll. On large boulders and on natural rock surfaces, however, this early type of art is as well represented in the peninsula as anywhere in Britain, there being no fewer than ninety groups of cup marks recorded, along with fifteen examples of cup and ring carvings; two groups of plain cup markings occurring on standing stones. No one has yet been able to apportion a particular purpose to this extremely early form of art or writing, whichever it was. Certainly the work of carrying it out must have been extremely arduous, so it is unlikely to have been done just for the fun of the thing.

The same complete mystery attaches itself to the purpose of the standing stones, of which there are no fewer than thirty-four in Kintyre. These are still referred to, here and there as 'Druid Stones', though they are unlikely to have had any connection with the Druids, no record of whom appears until, as priests of the Gauls, a full thousand years after most of these great stones had been set up. As has been said, a few bear carvings; some have been roughly shaped, while others bear not a trace of hewing of any sort. Their siting gives rise to theories of their use in religious rites, burial practices, and even solar and stellar observation connected with the fixing of the seasons. There is strong evidence to support the latter theory, but since the people who had those monoliths erected either could not or purposefully did not desire to leave any carved record, the true purpose of the erect stones may never be ascertained. In Kintyre, the most impressive of these monuments is at Beacharr, in close proximity to the celebrated chambered cairn, and rising to a height of nearly 17ft.

Beyond any shadow of doubt, many relics of the Bronze Age lie buried in Kintyre, and many will yet come to light through chance peat-cutting, ploughing or building excavation. A rich collection of both pottery and bronze is on view in Campbeltown Museum. There are food vessels and cinerary urns, bronze fragments, spearheads, at least one flat axe, a riveted knife and awl, several very beautifully worked socketed axes, a sword and fragments of other swords, a beautiful necklace of jet and other articles.

IRON AGE (600 BC TO AD 400)

It is impossible to say exactly when the first articles of iron reached Kintyre. Certainly it was during this last thousand years before Christ, when what we now speak of as refugees were on the march across Europe, in flight westward from the warlike hordes which swept across the continent from farther east.

Many of those fleeing tribes would never have reached Britain, since they would be over-run and in many cases massacred, only chosen slaves and women being carried forward with the onrush of the conquering war bands.

Here again, there can be no clear-cut date line between one metal age and the next; for, certainly during this thousand years of European unrest, the first of the war bands to reach Britain, and eventually Kintyre, did carry swords and other weapons of the Late Bronze Age. A few actually rode in wheeled chariots drawn by a small breed of horse. They very likely introduced the earliest horses to Kintyre, where the animal was so enthusiastically adopted and so widely bred that when Ptolemy came to make his map of North Britain he bestowed on the Mull the Greek equivalent of the name 'Headland of the Horse', and gave the inhabitants the tribal name of *Epidi*—horse people.

Long before this time, of course, further waves of armed war bands had appeared and conquered—their victories made easier, in the last few hundred years BC, by the discovery that iron, which was much more readily obtainable than bronze, could very quickly arm a whole band rather than only a few members of it. Iron swords and spears must have been to the beautiful old bronze weapons as the maxim gun was to the muzzle-loading smooth bore musket.

In Kintyre, relics of Iron Age occupation are confined mainly to the large number of earthworks and defensive buildings of stone known as duns, or forts. Generally speaking, all duns, that is, protective walls of stone usually occupying an eminence, were also forts. The distinction offered by the Royal Commission on the Ancient and Historical Monuments of Scotland, of 1971, is the very simple and satisfactory one that, while both were defensive structures, a fort might be regarded as one large enough to contain a small community, while a dun, even of similar structure, would be expected to serve the defensive needs of only one family. Well distributed throughout the peninsula are approximately sixty-five duns and twenty-four larger structures which can be termed forts.

Only a very few of these have so far been excavated other than by stone robbers. The most interesting are perhaps the vitrified stronghold at Carradale, already mentioned, and the dun so commandingly sited at Dun Skeig, where portions of an earlier stoneworks show evidence of having been moved at some later date to extend or strengthen a newer fortification.

These duns, though classed as of Iron Age construction, probably continued to be built and used in defence, as garrisoned posts of invading conquerors or as look-out or beacon-towers, for several hundreds of years—in a few cases right down to the Middle Ages, when they would have been manned against cattle raiders and other marauders.

As has been stated, very little excavation has as yet been carried out on forts and duns in Kintyre. Such meagre finds as have been made range in date from roughly 300 BC into the second century AD and early Christian times.

All this while, coming and going between Kintyre and nearby Ireland went on, and increased, though there was little if any contact with South Britain, soon to fall under Roman occupation. The Romans never did reach Kintyre, but it is extremely likely that keen eyes watched Agricola's fleet when, in AD 82, it passed the Mull on its voyage round the Scottish coast.

By now, methods of farming and fishing in Kintyre were improving under the integration of the varied peoples who had arrived and settled there down the centuries. Their dwellings were still primitive in the extreme, and such laws as they had inclined to be tribal and barbarous. Recorded history, as concerns Kintyre, was in the throes of being born. It came, in AD 498, with the arrival from Ireland of the three sons of Erc, to found the new kingdom of Dalriada.

Page 35   (above) The end of the road. The narrow way corkscrews dizzily down towards the Mull of Kintyre; (below) curious rock formation near Skipness gives the impression of being 'wind-blown' over the centuries

CAMPBELTOWN MAIL COACH.

CAMPBELTOWN MOTOR MAIL.

Page 36   Old Kintyre: (*left*) The
beginnings of mechanisation in the
carriage of mail; (*below*) a dwelling
of the type no longer found anywhere in Kintyre

3 A THOUSAND YEARS OF HISTORY

WHERE an undisputed happening stands clear from the mists of legend, there begins the history of a people. The history of Kintyre, which is the history of Scotland—of the United Kingdom even—can thus be said to date from a day in AD 574, when the Christian missionary Columba placed the crown on the head of one Aidan, son of Gabhran, and declared him King of Dalriada, land of the Scots.

Never, till that day, had a king anywhere in the British Isles been given Christian blessing with his crown. The event, historically indisputable, is veiled by the thin haze of tradition only in respect of where, in Argyll, this coronation actually took place. Some authorities come down on the side of Dunadd, that hill fortress of the earliest Scots just north of Lochgilphead. Others point out that Aidan was more likely to have been crowned in that other Scots stronghold, Dunaverty, in the south of Kintyre, since he was of the direct line of Fergus, eldest of the three sons of Erc, whose original portion of the newly founded kingdom was southern Kintyre, where Tirfergus, 'the land of Fergus', bears his name to this day.

A controversy of even less consequence surrounds the throne on which Aidan sat for the ceremony. Bardic tradition, which cannot be lightly disregarded, is agreed that he sat on a certain block of stone on which earlier Dalriadic kings had been enthroned; and that this stone had been carried by the Scots from Ireland, with the blessing on it that the line of Erc would continue to reign wherever it rested.

Undoubtedly, such a stone *was* part of the enthronement

c

37

ceremony when Kenneth MacAlpin became first king of the united Scots and Picts in 843. It was removed—with the centre of government—first to Dunstaffnage near Oban and later to Scone in Perthshire. Known as the Stone of Destiny, it was a sufficiently important part of the regalia of Scotland for Edward I of England to insist on carrying it off, with other plunder, to his own capital.

Now, while everyone knows that the block of stone borne south by Edward is as likely as not to be the one still in Westminster, some disagreement exists over its having been the real Stone of Destiny. Was the Saxon overlord fobbed off with a lump of rock which bears all the marks of having been quarried no nearer to Ireland or Kintyre than Perthshire? If so, as seems likely enough, the hiding place of the original has yet to be uncovered. And the ancient prophecy has held good down the centuries; for, though there may be many a bend in the long line, it was a queen in descent of Fergus Mac Erc and of Aidan of Dalriada who was enthroned on the present stone at Westminster in 1953.

Argyll had known those people who were called Scots for a couple of centuries before Fergus Mac Erc founded his kingdom in Kintyre towards the beginning of the sixth century. A colony of them appears to have been established, arriving from Ireland under their leader, Cairbre, around the year 258. This Cairbre, known in Ireland as *Righ fada*, the tall king, had already carved out a small kingdom for himself in Antrim, which was called *Dail Righ fhada*—pronounced Dalriada—and meaning just the 'portion of the tall king'. This name he gave also to the territories wrested from the Picts in what is now Mid Argyll and Kintyre, but from which his descendants were forced to retreat to Ireland after six generations. Two generations later, however, in 498, Cairbre's direct descendants, the three sons of Erc, gained a new foothold in Dalriada—this time to stay.

These rulers of the new Kingdom of Scotland appear to have divided the occupied territory amicably enough between them. Angus, youngest of the three, was given sovereignty of the isles of Jura and Islay, his stronghold being Dun Naomhaig, later called Dunyveg, on Islay. The race of Lorn, the next brother, occupied the area still known as Lorn, in northern Argyll, with his chief stronghold as the castle of Dunolaigh—now Dunolly—near Oban.

From a variety of chronicles, it seems clear that, though these two administered their allotted territories, they acknowledged their elder brother, Fergus Mor, as king of all the race. King Fergus, whose immediate possession appears to have been the fruitful land of South Kintyre, reigned for only three years. His son, named Domnagart, succeeded him, followed by his grandson Comgall who is recorded as having reigned for twenty-four years without battle. Comgall's brother Gabhran—king for twenty-two years—was the father of Aidan who was proclaimed king of Scots by Columba.

AIDAN TO SOMERLED

Aidan died in 605 after a thirty-four-year reign of wide ranging battles, from all of which he appears, from Annals of Ulster and other sources, to have emerged victorious.

Stormy times followed for Dalriada, which—out of the confusion that exists among records of kingly succession—seems clearly to have come for a long time under domination of the Britons of Strathclyde.

Out of all the welter of disagreement, one fact emerges clear; the line of Fergus Mor, son of Erc, continued to reign. It is probable that the warlike Picts overran and repossessed large areas. It is even possible that the two peoples lived peaceably, at times, and intermarried. At any rate, there are no grounds for disbelieving the learned investigators who hold that Alpin, father of Kenneth I, who became king over the united Picts and Scots in 853, had for his wife a princess of the Pictish race.

For at least half a century before this time, Kintyre had been the object of Norse raids. The Scots seat of government was moved far from the turbulent area; the peninsula would appear to have been abandoned to a settling down period that was to last for four centuries.

The Norse raiders established their own settlements, especially along the sheltered east coast of the peninsula where place names like Torrisdale, Smerby, Uigle, Borgadale and Skipness remain as memorials of their occupation. They would seem to have integrated with the Scots of Kintyre and by the end of the eleventh century became almost one people of a mixed race. They were known to the mainland Celts as *Gall Gaidheil*— foreign Gaels—and took part in the Norse cause against the Irish, at the great battle of Clontarf in 1014.

Kintyre might well have become a peaceful part of the Scottish kingdom from then on, but for the increasing demands of a greedy Norwegian overlordship embracing the isles from Man to the Hebrides—and with longing eyes always on Kintyre, which their king, Magnus II, described as 'best of all the isles excepting only Man'.

The Scottish king, Edgar, son of Malcolm Canmore, was glad enough to be rid of territory that yielded him no revenue anyway and in the Treaty of Tarbert ceded to Magnus all the isles—an island being defined as any land round which a ship could sail. The date of this treaty was 1098. Magnus ratified it instantly—by having a ship drawn overland across the narrow isthmus of Tarbert, its sails set and himself seated at the helm. Thus was Kintyre declared an island within the meaning of the act—as no doubt the wily Magnus, known as the Barefoot, pointed out.

This new king of Kintyre got off to a bad start by dispossessing many of the established *Gall Gaidheil* chiefs—among them, one Gillibride of the ancient line of Dalriada and father of the later famous warrior, Somerled, whose descendants were to have more influence on Kintyre's history and on the history of Scotland than any other family.

On the death of Magnus, five years after his annexing of Kintyre, Somerled emerged from the fastnesses of Morvern and, rallying the remnants of the *Gall Gaidheil*, drove the usurpers utterly from Kintyre and the isles, of which area he himself was now acknowledged king.

The kings of Scotland, in the meantime, appear to have pretended that neither Magnus nor Somerled existed, and that Kintyre was not, in fact, a part of their realm. When David I founded Holyrood Abbey in 1128, he blithely bestowed on it, as part of its endowment, one half of his tithes and revenue from Kintyre and Argyll. The remaining half, he presently bestowed on the Abbey of Dunfermline, with the proviso that the money would be paid over when he himself received it—a fairly clear indication that the Scottish exchequer was not then in receipt of any revenue from Kintyre.

Somerled was prepared to go a deal farther on his assertion of independent kingship; in 1164, he headed an army in defiance of Malcolm IV, and was slain in the ensuing battle at Renfrew on the Clyde.

A tomb in the long-ruined Abbey of Saddell is pointed out as Somerled's. Certainly his son Reginald, who reigned in his stead, is buried there. Reginald is usually credited with the foundation of Saddell, but Somerled himself may actually have been the founder. The thirteenth century, soon to begin, saw the ancient Celtic church of Iona give way, in Kintyre, to the Church of Rome, to which Reginald and his successors gave generous support, not only in the sustenance of the Cistercian Abbey at Saddell, but with liberal gifts of cattle and money to the monks of Paisley.

This preoccupation with religious matters was most likely the factor which led to Reginald's grandson, Angus Mor, son of Donald, becoming, in 1266, the first of Somerled's line to admit the right of Alexander III of Scotland to kingship of Kintyre also. He retained the style Lord of Islay assumed by Reginald, but became such a trusted supporter of the Scottish crown that, as one of the great barons of the kingdom, he had a seat in that parliament which, in 1284, settled the crown on the Maid of Norway.

THE BRUCE

Angus Og—young Angus—succeeded his father. This is the chief of Somerled's line who came out strongly for Robert Bruce in the disputed claim for the crown of Scotland. Angus not only gave the Bruce refuge at his castle of Dunaverty in South Kintyre, but contrived the king's escape to hiding in Rathlin, and later led a strong force of Highlanders to the decisive victory at Bannockburn.

That the undisputed king of an independent Scotland would wish to show his gratitude to such a loyal supporter as Angus Og is understandable. The manner in which the Bruce marked his favour might, however, strike some readers of history as a trifle backhanded. What the king did was to grant to Angus the forfeited estates of the MacDougalls of Lorn in northern Argyll; which grant, Angus might be said to have earned. At the same time, Bruce dispossessed Angus of his ancestral lands of Kintyre and invested them in his own nephew, Robert the Steward.

It can only be concluded that Robert Bruce, who was nobody's fool, had observed, in his fugitive wanderings in Kintyre, that Somerled's heirs were still virtually monarchs there. His determination to assume personal kingship of this hitherto debatable corner of his realm is demonstrated in his re-enactment of Magnus Barefoot's ship-dragging method of annexing the territory, as described by his biographer, the poet Barbour:

> And quhen thai that in the Ilis war,
> Herd tell how the gud Kyng had thar,
> Gert schippis with the salys ga,
> Out-our betwuix the Tarbartis twa,
> Thai war absit utrely,

For thai wist throu ald prophesy,
That he that suld ger schippis swa,
Betuix the seis with salis ga,
Suld syn the Ilis swa till hand,
That nane withsthrynth suld him withstand.

In addition to this symbolic voyage, which he knew well would deeply impress his Gaelic subjects, the Bruce took the more practical step of rebuilding the castle at Tarbert. This strategically placed fortress is of great antiquity. Almost certainly built by Fergus, the son of Erc, it had probably fallen into ruin after being burned by Sealbach of Lorn in 712 and by his son Dungal nineteen years later.

In the oldest extant exchequer roll of Scotland, compiled by John de Lany, whom Bruce installed as Constable of Tarbert, the accounts of monies spent on the castle's restoration are preserved in detail. Not unexpectedly, the highest payment went to the stonemason, whose name was Robert, and who was given—in addition to the contracted sum of £282 15s, a chalder of oatmeal and the same of barley—a bonus of £5 for making the wall thicker than he had agreed to do. The smith, named Neil, had £12 for a year's work, the carpenter and the plumber earned 3d and 8d per day respectively—the former having an allowance of meal and cheese to even matters up. The chaplain must surely have had other income to supplement the 15s paid to him as half a year's salary. That the king took a close personal interest in the work of restoration is clear from the number of payments made by his personal instruction; and the agreement with one William Scott for the construction of the moat was actually signed in the king's presence. The cost of the entire work on the castle amounted to about £511.

There is no record of Angus Og becoming any less royalist after the seeming slight of having to surrender his ancient rights in Kintyre. His son, John, may well have plotted to recover these. At any rate, John, by judicious marriage with Amie MacRuari, soon acquired title to the isles, of which she was heiress. He at once assumed the style of Lord of the Isles—Dominus de Insularum—which was to be held by his three successors. Later, when the time was opportune, he divorced Amie, and replaced her by Margaret Stewart, daughter of the man who was by then Robert II of Scotland—that Robert on whom his uncle, the late king, had bestowed the lands of Kintyre taken away from Angus Og. In 1377, Robert II formally bestowed the lands on John, Lord of the Isles and his lady Margaret. It had not taken long for Kintyre to return to possession of the line of Somerled, whose representatives had now a firmer hold of it than ever before.

LORDSHIP OF THE ISLES

There followed a full century in which the Lords of the Isles ruled in Kintyre practically as independent kings of a state apart from Scotland. They had their own laws, appointed their own judges, maintained their own army and navy, and actually dealt with the English monarchy as a separate power. Successive Stewart kings of Scotland, beginning with the first James, each made efforts to bring the proud lordship to the royal heel, an object which not all would agree was completely achieved even when James IV finally dispossessed John—also fourth Lord of the Isles—in 1493. Before that, the power of the mighty lordship had already been in eclipse when the earldom of Ross was forfeited from John of the Isles seventeen years earlier.

During their long rule in Kintyre, these MacDonald lords—they had been the sons of Donald since the far-off days of John Mor, son of Donald who was grandson of Somerled—had naturally invested the best lands in branches of their own family. The most powerful emerged as the MacDonalds of Dun Naomhaig, or Dunyveg, from their fortress of that name in Islay. This branch of the family was styled 'of Islay and Kintyre' and was also known as *Clann Iain Mhoir*—the race of big John—from their descent from John Mor Tanister, brother of the second Lord of the Isles. Before the final dissolution of the ancient lordship, James III had begun a process of reducing MacDonald power in Kintyre, first by creating the sheriffdom of Tarbert, with power invested in the constable of his castle there, ranging over northern Kintyre. In the same year, 1481, he declared South Kintyre a stewardry, which amounted to much the same thing, since the appointed crown steward, who was given as his headquarters the ancient MacDonald stronghold of Dunaverty Castle, had all the powers of a sheriff of the king. For this appointment, James chose one Charles MacAllister of Loup—an estate on West Loch Tarbert with which the name was associated up to the nineteenth century.

James IV kept up the pressure, after the complete forfeiture of the lordship in 1493, by strengthening the fortifications of other castles on the peninsula, and by the installation therein of trusted servitors of his own choosing. The Castle of Skipness he entrusted to his comptroller, Sir Duncan Forestare, to whom he gave large grants of neighbouring land. The Castle of Ardcardle, or Airds Castle—of which only fragments of a curtain wall remain today—situated near Carradale on the east coast, was given with a grant of neighbouring lands to Sir Adam Reid, an Ayrshire laird and head of the family of that name.

Oddly enough, the king, while seemingly bent on the utter severance of the MacDonald hold on Kintyre, at the same time appears anxious not to break with that powerful family completely. On a visit to the Highlands in the summer of 1493, he held court at Dunstaffnage, and there honoured with the accolade of knighthood John Cathanach MacDonald, of Dun Naomhaig in Islay. It might not be surprising if the new knight took this favour as a hint that his lost Kintyre lands, together with the keepership of his family's ancient stronghold of Dunaverty, were soon to be returned to him.

Far from that being the king's intention, however, when James again visited Kintyre the following year, it was with no other purpose than to strengthen the fortification of Dunaverty, set new and better cannon in position, and install a governor of his own choosing.

The enraged MacDonald took instant action. With a determined band of his clan, he stormed the newly fortified castle, and hanged the scarcely appointed governor from its battlements in full sight of the astonished king, who, attended by only a small bodyguard, was just putting off by boat, for his ship. It was the final wild gesture of the line of Somerled—though Kintyre had not yet heard the last of them. John Cathanach and his sons made their escape to the fastnesses of the Glens of Antrim, where they had loyal kin through a marriage of a brother of Donald, the second lord, with the heiress of that estate. Royal and terrible retribution overtook them a few years later, when John Cathanach and at least two of his sons were betrayed, captured and hanged on the one gallows. King James IV could now sleep soundly, sure that the lordship of the isles was broken, and that he reigned undisputed in Kintyre.

The king's preoccupation with this hitherto debatable corner of his realm is made clear in a further royal visit to Kintyre in 1498, when he set about the erection of a new castle, that of Kilkerran, of which only shattered remains stand today in a cottage garden not far from the modern town of Campbeltown. It was probably on this occasion that the king annexed the lands of the already long deserted Abbey of Saddell to the bishopric of Argyll, empowering the then bishop to build the formidable Castle of Saddell, which still stands well preserved nearby.

Another step the king took was in the appointment of Archibald, 2nd Earl of Argyll, as crown chamberlain of the confused lands of the forfeited lordship. This marked the thin end of a Campbell wedge which was to widen its hold in Kintyre up to the twentieth century. It was in July of 1505, that the earl—later to fall with his king at Flodden—arrived at the straggling village and principal town, at the south of the peninsula, known by the awkward name of Ceann Loch Cille Chiaran—the head of the loch of Ciaran's Chapel. Here, with characteristic thoroughness, he prepared a set of accounts for all the crown lands of Kintyre, with the names and extent of the holdings, the annual value of each, and the names of the occupants. This, the earliest Kintyre rental, remains a document of the principal families of the sixteenth century, some of whose descendants occupy the same lands today.

The Earl of Argyll had already brought in the new name of Campbell by obtaining from Sir Duncan Forestare the lands of Skipness. The Campbell hold tightened when, later that century, Argyll became superior of all the former Iona church lands of what is now Kilchenzie, followed by a similar superiority over the lands of Macharioch and Sanda, till then a part of the Priory of Whithorn in Galloway. It was not until the beginning of a new century, in 1607, that Campbell domination of Kintyre became complete when the 7th Earl of Argyll finally obtained the grant of all the lands of the forfeited lordship of the isles.

An act of the Scottish parliament, ten years earlier, had settled the chief conditions of the grant of these lands to Argyll. Briefly, it amounted to the setting up of a lowland burgh of lowland burgesses at the principal town, whose name was by now shortened and anglicised to Lochhead, and the planned colonisation of Kintyre by lowland families. On his own shrewd initiative, Argyll also planned to bring in various other Campbell families from the mainland of Argyll. Colonisation—or plantation, as it was called—was not an entirely new method of bringing calm to turbulent areas. Already, a plan to 'plant' the Isle of Lewis with families from Fife had failed. Ulster, too, was in process of being colonised by Scots and English. The colonisation of Kintyre just happened to be part of the policy of the time. It might have been expected to bring peace to a long troubled Kintyre at last. That it did not do so was— it should be said—no fault of the lowland colonists. There were old Highland scores to be settled yet, in Argyll.

4   KINTYRE UNDER THE CAMPBELLS

GILLEASBUIG GRUAMACH, or Archibald the Grim, 7th Earl of Argyll, had been entrusted with a task for which the time was not yet ripe. His monarch, James VI of Scotland and I of England, looked to the seemingly rich unexploited resources of the West Highlands as a means of bolstering his dwindling economy. Archibald himself was far from being without his own money difficulties. So, doubtless with the replenishment of his own coffers as a stimulus, he set about the task of erecting the planned burgh in Kintyre.

As an opening act, in 1609, he put in hand the building of a new fortress, the Castle of Lochhead, which was to be the dominant structure of the future town. Oddly enough, not the remotest trace remains of this, the most modern fortalice in all Kintyre. It must have stood on that high part of the present town, still called Castlehill, probably on the site occupied today by the police station. In addition, the earl is believed to have laid out the Main Street, running steeply down to the harbour.

PLANTATION

At the same time, he opened the colonisation by granting the feu of lands, including what is now Dalintober and Dalaruan, to one John Boyll of Kelburn, conferring on him also the right to distil 'aquavitae'. This license to distil spirit was the fore-runner of an industry which was to bring much wealth to the burgh of a later day.

It is of interest to note that in this first charter, dated at Inverary in April 1609, the agreed feu-duty is laid down as payable annually 'at the castle or fortalice of Keanloch Kilcheran to be built beside the toune of Campbeltoune'. This would seem to make clear that, by that date, the earl had already gone ahead with at least some of the town buildings, though not yet the castle. It also points to his decision to perpetuate his name in that of the new town—which, however, was never referred to other than by its original Ceann Loch Cille Chiaran, or the English version Lochhead, for at least another seventy years.

That he did build the castle very soon afterwards is certain; this was watched from afar by the MacDonalds, who had not taken the forfeiture of their lordship as the final word.

A certain Sir James MacDonald—a direct descendant of that John Cathanach who had stormed Dunaverty and hanged the newly installed governor before the astonished eyes of James IV—had been long held prisoner in Edinburgh, for a time under sentence of execution. The intricate political intrigues of the early seventeenth century are hard to unravel now, but there is a suspicion that James VI did not dare to confirm the sentence since Sir James's allegedly criminal activities had been carried on under the king's own seal.

Be that as it may, this Sir James MacDonald contrived a fairly easy escape from Edinburgh Castle in 1615, rallied the sons of Donald in the west, and captured by clever strategy the ancient stronghold of Dun Naomhaig in Islay. From there he sailed to Kintyre, sending the fiery cross before him, and seized and held what Gregory refers to as 'the King's Castle at Kinloch', that is, the newly built fortress of Argyll.

The Islay rebellion, as this foray came to be known, was, however, short-lived in its early success. MacDonald escaped capture, fled to Ireland and ultimately to Spain.

In the meantime, perhaps not surprisingly, the Earl of Argyll's progress with the peaceful establishment of the projected lowland burgh was slow. His first countess had borne him the son who was to become the famed Marquis of Argyll; when she died, he married an English lady of the Catholic faith. It is probable that his subsequent unpredictable behaviour stemmed from the influence of this second countess.

King James clearly held the earl in high esteem, for he it was who was chosen to bear the royal crown when that monarch performed the state opening of parliament in Edinburgh in June of 1617. Soon afterwards, he obtained leave from the king to repair to the Well of Spa, to take the water there. It is unlikely that his health was in any way suspect, for no sooner had he got overseas than he embraced the Catholic religion of his countess. To the further rage of his erstwhile royal patron, he entered the military service of the king of Spain. Less than two years after his glittering performance at the state opening of parliament, the earl was put to the horn, that is, publicly, at the Mercat Cross of Edinburgh, with sound of trumpets, declared a rebel and traitor.

While in Spain, it is recorded, the earl met and conversed with his former arch enemy, Sir James MacDonald, who had, some years earlier, taken refuge in that country, after his abortive raiding in Kintyre and Islay. Incidentally, a year later, MacDonald was granted full pardon and summoned to return home by the king, who was narrowly prevented by his privy council from restoring the ancient MacDonald lordship in Kintyre. The advice of the council prevailed, and though MacDonald was granted a royal pension he never did return to Scotland, but died in London in 1626.

A year later, the Earl of Argyll was also pardoned, though he likewise never reached Scotland again. His lands in Kintyre, controlled in his absence by powerful Campbell cadets, were resigned to the keeping of his second son James, Lord Kintyre, who was entrusted anew—by charter of Charles I in 1626—with the already agreed plan for the colonisation of Kintyre.

This young man seems to have been of a bold, adventurous

spirit better suited to his successful exploits in pursuit of pirates then ravaging the Kintyre coasts than to the sober business of town planning. He had clearly decided, by 1635, to dispose of his responsibilities along with his estates; despite the clause in his charter from Charles I, expressly forbidding the transfer of land in Kintyre to any of the name of MacDonald, he was, in that year, in process of making over not only the lands of the Kintyre lordship, but those of Jura also, to the MacDonalds of Antrim, in the person of Viscount Dunluce, son of the first Earl of Antrim who belonged to the family of the MacDonalds of Dun Naomhaig.

The Privy Council of Scotland took instant action to prevent the ratification of the transfer before the MacDonalds could take up actual occupation, and Lord Kintyre resigned his lands to the crown, which promptly bestowed them on his brother, Lorne, shortly to become the one and only Marquis of Argyll.

Under the marquis, peaceful domestic settlement of Kintyre might have gone ahead smoothly enough, and there is recorded evidence of his industry in this direction in the accounts of the Regality of Argyll for that year, 1636. Yet, a strange quirk of fate was just around the corner. It was only three years before the first 'Bishops' War' found King Charles in armed conflict with his own subjects; and his first action was to invite the MacDonald Earl of Antrim to invade Argyll with the promise of the formerly fiercely denied lands of Kintyre as his reward.

The marquis was fully alive to the likelihood of such an invasion. To contest it suitably, he constructed a fortified earthworks or entrenchment on a point of land across the loch from the growing town, armed it with cannon and manned it with a considerable garrison under his kinsman of Auchinbreck. That war, in fact, fizzled to a temporary end inside of a year. It was followed, in 1641, by the uprising in Ireland that brought about a temporary reconciliation between King Charles and his subjects of Kintyre, who, under the marquis, fought in Ireland against the Earl of Antrim and others of the clan

Donald. Among them were Coll MacGillesbuig Mhic Coll MacDonald of the Dun Naomhaig branch and his sons, of which family more was to be heard yet, to the awful cost of Kintyre and all Argyll.

During this time, the fortified entrenchment was again manned. General Leslie found seven cannon still there, on his march to Dunaverty six years later. Today, the site is occupied by a thriving shipyard, but is still known by its name of Trench Point.

THE COLKITTO RAIDS

The civil war which has been spoken of as fizzling to a temporary end flared up, in Kintyre, in extremely bloody form, from 1644 on, as part of the greater struggle then being waged throughout the whole United Kingdom.

When, in that year, the great and famous Marquis of Montrose raised an army in support of Charles I, it was too good an opportunity for the MacDonald Earl of Antrim to miss. He dispatched a force of about 1,500 men to join Montrose, placing them under the command of Alasdair MacDonald of Colonsay, one of the several sons of the wily old Coll MacGillesbuig. This old man was an inveterate Campbell hater, and possibly not without reason. Being left-handed, or *ciotach*, in the Gaelic speech, he was known as Coll Ciotach. English chroniclers of the time could render this only as 'Colkitto', the dreaded name by which his better known and more feared son, Alasdair, goes down in history.

The colour of any character portrait of Alasdair MacDonald varies according to the painter. Sir James Turner, the historian who marched with the parliament forces of General Leslie, clearly hated MacDonald; he belittles his qualities as a leader and brands him as a besotted drunken despot. Royalist diarists of the time present a different picture, and certainly later historians, however grudgingly, have had to grant to Colkitto some of the heroic qualities ascribed to him by the enthusiastic

Page 53   (*above*) Kintyre harvesting of a more leisurely day; (*below*) the former tea-room at Machrihanish, now the village hall

Page 54 Ruins: (*above*) Sheep and lambs find shade as well as grazing in the burnt-out shell of the original Keil School. This famous school for boys, destroyed in 1924, was never rebuilt, but was housed, from that year, near to Dumbarton; (*below*) all that remains of the Bruce's Castle at Tarbert. Members of the local Scout Cubs practise, within its ruined curtain wall, an art well known to Scotland's hero king

Highlanders, largely Kintyre Royalists with MacDonald sympathies, who joined with Antrim's force in the Montrose campaigns. Somewhere between is the true picture of a man who at least appears to have displayed a quality of generalship often in advance of his time.

For more than a year MacDonald's forces were of signal service to the victorious Montrose, who was empowered by King Charles, after the battle of Kilsyth, to reward his lieutenant with the accolade of knighthood. It was about this time that MacDonald took the step which had probably been his aim since first landing in Scotland. He detached his own powerful army from that of Montrose, and proceeded to wage his own war against the Campbell clan in a last wild bid to restore to the race of Somerled the lost lordship of Kintyre and Islay.

When, presently, King Charles himself ordered Montrose to cease the struggle and avoid more bloodshed, MacDonald considered himself above the king's command. Later, General Leslie offered him amnesty on the condition of surrender; but this too MacDonald flatly refused, being now in rebellion against both king and parliament.

From this point began the series of wild forays known as the Colkitto Raids, during which MacDonald and his aged father, Coll Ciotach, rampaged through Argyll and Kintyre, with burning, sacking, pillage and slaughter. Montrose's victory at Inverlochy in 1645, in which MacDonald's forces had played a vital part, had thrown the Marquis of Argyll's army into utter confusion, and dropped Kintyre like a ripe plum for devouring by the rebel sons of Donald. By 1646 the whole peninsula had been reduced to a burnt desert, its cattle driven away, many of the people slain or fled, their houses blackened, smoking ruins.

By the end of that year, the marquis sought exemption from parliament for payment of feu-duties, since he himself had received no rents from his Kintyre lands for three years. Not only was this granted, but an act of parliament awarded him

D

£15,000 sterling in compensation for damage inflicted on his estates.

Meantime, the Covenanting forces under General Leslie were being regrouped and re-armed, with the object of crushing Colkitto's raiders once and for all. The first engagement of the attack took place at Gocumgow, where MacDonald chanced to be encamped for the night, not far from the ford at the south end of Lochawe. Little is known of this encounter, except that, from there, MacDonald withdrew speedily into Kintyre; even the sober historian Turner expresses astonishment over his tactical failure to hold the narrow isthmus—an operation which, seemingly easy to mount, would have utterly foiled General Leslie's Covenanting army. Why a general of Mac-Donald's admitted calibre failed in this obvious manoeuvre will never be known.

Where documented history is silent, tradition holds that the defence of the passes had been entrusted to the MacAllisters of Loup—one of the prominent Kintyre families known to have marched with MacDonald—and that, for some extraordinary reason, the MacAllisters preoccupied themselves with the siege of Skipness Castle, to the neglect of their appointed duty.

Surely something like this occurred, for it is certain that Leslie's cavalry, in the van of his army, passed right through the isthmus of Tarbert without opposition, followed by the foot, to surprise MacDonald's forces on the open ground of Kil-calmonell, a little to the south. The ensuing battle fought on the level moss of Rhunahaorine was bloody in the extreme, though causing little loss to Leslie's army, the main body of which had not yet even crossed the isthmus.

Mercifully, evening commanded disengagement. But the fate of the MacDonalds had been sealed. Sir Alasdair and his ageing father, Coll, escaped by boat, apparently having instructed their broken forces to retreat to the fortress of Dunaverty, where they might hold out till relief could be brought, possibly from Antrim.

The parliamentary army followed the retreating MacDonald forces down the peninsula, taking without opposition the Castle of Lochhead, where the Marquis of Argyll and General Leslie established their headquarters. Just before their arrival at the port, the Irish contingent appears to have escaped by sea, touching at Islay to pick up their leader.

The remnant of Sir Alasdair's now broken force, mostly Kintyre Highlanders and MacDougalls, under command of Archibald Mor MacDonald of Sanda, had already sought the refuge of Dunaverty's ancient walls, where Leslie's avenging army finally came up with them on or about 31 May. By now the number of men holding the keep had dwindled to a little over five hundred.

What followed has been variously reported. Turner avers that MacDonald had effected his own escape on a promise to return in force and relieve Dunaverty. There is strong local tradition that this promise was kept, and that an attempt at landing was bloodily repulsed. Human remains found among the sandy bunkers and on the beaches of Brunerican, to the east of the fortress, offer silent corroboration of this tale. But historians on the spot remain as silent as the bones. If indeed any attempt was made, it certainly failed in its purpose.

Dunaverty was a fortress already hoary with age. Probably founded by Fergus Mac Erc in the sixth century, it had been besieged by Sealbach of Lorn in 712, garrisoned by Alexander III against Haco of Norway in 1263, and was the refuge of Robert Bruce, in the safe hands of Angus Og in the dark days of 1306. By now, of course, it was officially and legally a possession of the Marquis of Argyll, Lord of Kintyre, who was determined to translate legality into fact.

Since Sir James Turner was the only historian on the spot, his version of the siege and its bloody end has to be depended on for the basic facts—though gruesome details he apparently overlooked were brought to light in evidence given at Argyll's trial fourteen years later.

The defence of the fortress depended on the holding of a runnel of water, probably a diversion from the Coniglen Burn, passing the outer defences, and guarded by a trench constantly manned by a party of the defenders. To Argyll's regiment fell the task of capturing this vital outpost, an object they accomplished with the loss of six killed, against forty dead of the desperately fighting besieged. From there on, it was only a matter of time—a much shorter time than some traditional accounts make out. The hot, sultry days of early June told their tale.

A consensus of evidence points to the date of the surrender as being about 10 June, when, after a parley conducted on the investing side by Turner himself, the garrison, which he numbered at about three hundred men, laid down their arms and came out.

It may or may not be true that the recorder of the subsequent events himself begged General Leslie to spare the lives of the vanquished. This is his story—and he certainly did successfully intercede for the life of one young man, John MacDougall of Dunolly, who was sent to France instead of being butchered by the Covenanting soldiers, as all the others had been.

There is little reliable evidence of what passed at the council held to decide the fate of the prisoners. At Argyll's subsequent trial, Turner asserted that while he had never heard the marquis urge Leslie to massacre the captives, John Nevay, the Presbyterian chaplain to the Covenanting army, had, with religious fanaticism, called down on the heads of both leaders all manner of curses from the almighty if they hesitated in their duty to slay all the heretic MacDonald rebels.

The bloody zeal of this clergyman prevailed over whatever soldierly misgivings General Leslie must surely have held. The order was given to put all the captives to the sword and the army literally hacked them to pieces. A few of the chiefs or officers, including MacDonald of Sanda and his son Archibald Og, were hanged or shot, or both. The scene on Dunaverty's rock that day, when 300 defenceless men were butchered in cold blood, can have few parallels in Scottish history.

As for Coll Ciotach and his distinguished son, their time was also running out. Old Coll, now about seventy-seven, was taken by Leslie's triumphant forces at Dun Naomhaig, handed over to Argyll, tried by a Campbell jury and hanged on a makeshift scaffold, formed by the mast of his own galley placed across a narrow gully between the rocks. Two of his sons were also executed, one at Dun Naomhaig, the other at Skipness. Sir Alasdair was killed in Ireland later in that fatal year. The last, wild escapade of the race of Somerled had been played out.

Dunaverty, on its bloodstained rock, brooded in the silence that fell on it from that dreadful day. Thirty-eight years later, it was razed to the ground when the vengeful hordes of Atholl were, on the express orders of the solemn privy council, turned loose to destroy all of Argyll's castles, as well as to inflict all manner of barbarity on any known to have espoused the cause of the earl of that day.

DIVIDED LOYALTIES

The peace that, following the end of the Colkitto Raids, should have settled on Kintyre was short lived. Contrary to what might have been expected, the Covenanting party had not favoured the execution of Charles I. They promptly defied the English parliament by crowning his son at Scone, on New Year's Day of 1651, having first subjected him to what was regarded as a sufficient degree of admonition and preaching by ministers of the Covenant. The Marquis of Argyll himself placed the crown on the head of Charles II. Despite the preaching and admonitions, the king was still unable to satisfy all the leaders of the Covenant that his professions of their beliefs were sincere. As events were to prove, these misgivings were far from ill judged.

September 1651 saw Charles II's army routed at Worcester,

and the king in flight to the Continent. The Marquis of Argyll, for reasons of his own, presently not only recognised Cromwell's party, but entered into active collaboration with the English government. His son, later to become Earl of Argyll, opposed him violently, as did his own chamberlain in Kintyre, Mac-Nachtan of Dunderave. These two, under command of Lord Kenmore, headed a military expedition into Kintyre in 1653 and once again there was bloodshed and burning roofs. An expeditionary force of Cromwell's army had earlier attempted to land in Kintyre, from Ayr, but had been easily turned back. Indeed, only the Marquis of Argyll's personal intervention prevented every man, from their commander down, being slaughtered.

Lord Kenmore's royalist force was opposed, in Kintyre, by many of the principal lowland lairds who, under the plantation scheme, had already settled there. Most of these, like their leader, William Ralston, were fanatical Covenanters, and had doubtless been chosen as colonists for that as much as for any other reason. Therefore it is a reflection on the divided loyalties of the times that Ralston and other lowland gentlemen of Kintyre, all fervent Covenanters, now armed themselves on the side of the English government—to which the marquis had already gone over—in opposition to the absent king, in whose person they had not so long before invested the defence of their faith.

Kenmore's march into Kintyre might well have led to the wholesale hanging of these lowland lairds, but for the personal influence of Lorne, the marquis's son, who was a firm believer in the future of the estates that would one day be his, and knew well the value of perpetuating the lowland plantations.

The Restoration of 1660 brought short-lived joy to the Covenanters. One of Charles II's first acts was to bring to the execution block the Marquis of Argyll who had been the one to place the crown on his head. The king then proceeded to legislation for the enforcement of Episcopacy in a manner that, compared with any previous laws on religious observance, was as hard as iron is to milk and water.

By royal proclamation of this king who had once signed the Covenant, all ministers ordained over the past twelve years were commanded to submit their ordination to the rule of the bishops or be deprived of their livings. In the west of Scotland, 271 ministers refused and were immediately turned out, neck and crop with their families, to wander wheresoever they might.

In Kintyre itself, only three of the parishes had ministers at this date; all three refused to make submission and were turned out. From 1661 to 1687, therefore, the Presbyterian synod of Argyll went out of existence. In the latter year, when, under the new Act of Indulgence, it was convened at Glassary, it was found that, out of forty-five parishes, only six ministers remained.

Episcopalian curates, many of them ignorant and totally unlettered, were installed in their places. Yet, such country people as refused to attend the services held by these supplanters were subjected to heavy fines, which were extorted by soldiers sent about the country for the purpose. It was the day of the secret conventicle in fields or in hollows of the hills, with sentries set to watch for the soldiers of the fanatically Episcopal king.

The 9th Earl of Argyll, who had succeeded the executed marquis, had to watch his step carefully. He, too, had been condemned to the block in 1662, then had his estates restored to him the following year.

Known Covenanters in Kintyre, again principally lairds of the lowland plantation, were kept under strict watch by the government. The Earl of Argyll was given what must, to him, have been the somewhat distasteful task of arresting a number of these, including William Ralston, who was imprisoned at Dumbarton. Colonel James Wallace, who was also on his list, escaped to the lowlands to lead the so-called Pentland Rising, after which he had to make his escape to Holland.

The earl himself, whether with reason or not, was clearly not trusted by the government, which kept such a close eye on Kintyre that an uneasy peace reigned there. This was so marked that the planned immigration of lowland families was speeded up by the influx of refugees from the cruelly persecuted areas of nearby Ayr and Renfrew. Indeed, so many lowland families sought refuge in Kintyre between 1665 and 1683 that a state amounting almost to famine prevailed there. These families were not selected, as had been the case for the growing burgh of Lochhead after 1609 or by invitation to lowland lairds in the years following the Colkitto Raids. But the movement completed the repopulation of Kintyre, laid waste by these raids and by the plague which followed; and Kintyre today is populated by the descendants of those people, with a thin mixture of the ancient race of the *Gall Gaidheil*.

THE FINAL REBELLION

In 1681, the Earl of Argyll refused to subscribe to the Test Act, and was declared a traitor, tried and once more sentenced to the block. Awaiting execution at Edinburgh Castle, he escaped by a trick and made his way to Holland, where, foregathering with the Duke of Monmouth already in exile there, he took part in the hatching of the plot later known as the Monmouth Rising. This plot to topple the papist King James need never have taken place, since all that the rebels aimed for, involving much spilling of blood, was accomplished only three years later, when the protestant King William was welcomed ashore at Torbay.

From the start, Argyll's part in the rising was ill-starred. Sailing from Holland on 2 May 1685, with three small ships, the earl touched at Orkney and Islay before landing in Kintyre, where he hoped to rally much support from among the sworn Covenanters there. This support was not, however, forthcoming in the expected measure.

Before the ancient cross, which now stands near the quay but which in those times stood farther up the main street of the burgh, near the castle, the earl, with a flourish of trumpets, caused to be read a 'Declaration and Apology of the Protestant people . . . for defence and relief of their lives Rights and Liberties . . .' The declaration was 'Printed at Campbell-town in Kintyre, in the shire of Argyle. Anno. 1685'.

The response to the earl's call to arms in Kintyre was disappointing. It may be that the Covenanting lowlanders of Kintyre had had their fill of wars. Also, they had little reason to trust Argyll, who had never shown himself a fervent Covenanter; on the contrary, he had stamped heavily on those who had taken part in the Pentland Rising—the same people he expected to join him now.

At all events, news of the Monmouth plot had leaked from Holland. When the earl, with such forces as he could muster, left Campbeltown and eventually landed on the coast of Renfrew, it seems clear that he was expected. For there he was at once taken prisoner, brought to Edinburgh and marched straight to the execution block without the formality of a second trial.

Forthwith, the Privy Council of Scotland sent to Atholl those orders which have been called since, 'Letters of Fire and Sword'—the council's recognised mode of dealing with a rebellious clan by giving, against it, a licence of barbarity to a known enemy.

Part of the orders to Atholl read:

Meanwhile destroy what you can to all who joined any manner of way with him. All men who joined, and are not come off on your or Breaalbane's advertisement are to be killed or disabled ever from fighting again; and burn all homes except honest men's, and destroy Inverara and all the castles; and what you cannot undertake, leave to those who come after you to do . . . Let the women and children be transported to remote isles.

Once more Kintyre felt the scorching breath of fire and sword —not only at the hands of the barbaric Atholl raiders but, beneath their cloak, by bands of lawless robbers. All that dreadful summer of 1685, those ravening bands pillaged Kintyre, where conditions bordering on famine had been worsened by the influx of lowlanders, who now bore the brunt of their excesses. The revolution of three years later, with the beginning of King William's reign and the reinstatement of the family of Argyll in the person of the 10th Earl, brought about a public investigation and a scheme of compensation for those who had suffered by the wave of robbery.

Kintyre was emerging as an important area of a realm struggling out of the mists of bloody intrigue. The final and most eventful step in this direction was taken on 14 June 1700, when the inhabitants of what was now to be known as Campbeltown were summoned to the Tolbooth to hear the reading of the charter granted by King William. This raised their town to the status of Royal Burgh and conferred upon them the lieges of Campbeltown, the liberties and privileges that went therewith, which liberties and privileges they were to enjoy for all time 'freely, quietly, fully, entirely, honourably, rightly and in peace, without any impediment, revocation, contradiction or hindrance soever'.

OLD FAMILIES

Some who listened must surely have pondered on the magic in the name of Campbell; though even then well distributed in Kintyre, it was not and is still not an old one in the peninsula. Far the oldest name of note is MacDonald, represented by the MacDonalds of Largie, who are in direct descent from Somerled and, through him, of Fergus, eldest of the three sons of Erc.

MacEachern, another ancient name still found in Kintyre, must be regarded as amongst the oldest—probably dating from prehistoric times when the tribal name of the inhabitants of the peninsula was 'people of the horse'. MacEachern, in its earliest Gaelic form, can be translated as 'Son of the Lord of the Horse'. The name figures on the famous Campbeltown Cross which is believed to date from around 1380.

64

MacMurchy is another ancient name, its bearers being the sons of Murchadh, who was at one time musician, bard or minstrel to an early branch of the house of Donald. MacNeill, MacNair, MacOnohe—now McConnachie—are just a very few of the names long associated with the past history of Kintyre.

With the MacAllisters and the MacKinnons, the MacNeills are among those who have held land in Kintyre from very early times. McGilchrists and McKerrals are seldom to be met with outside the peninsula—save, perhaps in the United States and Canada, where natives of Kintyre, among the very earliest emigrants from these shores, played leading parts in the growth of nations which, out of the pioneering days, have emerged among the great powers of the world.

Yet, old families or new, the people of Kintyre stood united, that day in June 1700, at the end of eleven hundred years of their peninsula's story; united at the beginning of a new chapter to which they could look forward with the old feuds, old ills put behind them for ever.

5   POPULATION AND EMPLOYMENT

COMPARATIVE population figures for the whole peninsula are readily enough available over a very long period from *The Third Statistical Account*, of 1791, though these are difficult to analyse with any degree of accuracy, due to the changes in the boundaries of Campbeltown, where the population was always most dense, and in parish boundaries in cases where unions were brought into effect over the years.

Over the past century, however, precise figures are available and, with the turn of the present century, an overall downward trend will be noted. Figures for Campbeltown are given separately from the landward area of the parish in which it stands. Incidentally, Campbeltown continued to house the highest population of any town in Argyll until 1921, in which year Dunoon edged in front and has since maintained that position.

Parish	*1851*	*1901*	*1911*	*1931*	*1951*	
Southend	1,406	732	767	640	522	levelling
Campbeltown (Landward)	2,501	1,950	1,872	1,619	1,572	levelling
Killean & Kilchenzie	2,219	1,078	1,019	870	705	levelling
Saddell & Skipness	1,504	1,087	964	946	932	levelling
Kilcalmonell (inc part of Tarbert)	—	1,915	1,712	1,360	1,364	levelling
Gigha & Cara	547	374	326	243	190	Still falling
Burgh of Campbeltown	—	8,286	7,625	6,309	7,152	(6,045 in 1971)

LIVING FROM THE LAND

As largely today as when Somerled first wrested control of the peninsula from the Norsemen, the main economy of the whole community springs from its warm, fertile land.

The large creamery established in comparatively recent years on the site of one of Campbeltown's old distilleries is in a constant state of expansion, handling at present an annual 5 million gallons of milk from 162 lush dairy farms, processing and exporting its product in varying forms.

Nor is dairy produce the sole agricultural aim in Kintyre. Natural soil and geographic conditions combined, from earliest times, towards living from the land, but it cannot be forgotten that the present very high standard of farming had a painful and protracted birth, evolving out of trials and errors lasting over a period of some three hundred years from the granting to the 7th Earl of Argyll of the forfeited lands of the broken MacDonald lordship.

The Colkitto Raids of 1644–7 followed by General Leslie's bloody expedition would have been enough in themselves to leave a land of blackened rafters and desolate unseeded fields. Such devastation as pillaging troops of both armies failed to achieve was accomplished in the year after the Dunaverty massacre by the outbreak of bubonic plague which left large areas of the peninsula utterly desolated.

Various traditional accounts of the visitation of this pestilence survive. Peter MacIntosh in his *History of Kintyre* speaks of having been told in his youth of how 'the plague came from Ayr to Dunaverty in a white cloud, and spread over most of Kintyre. In a short time, the ravages it made were dreadful, turning the houses into graves, and multitudes fleeing for their lives . . .'

More recent evidence, however, points to the likelihood of the plague having been brought into Kintyre in 1647 by General

67

Leslie's armies, which had recently marched from the already infested areas around Dunkeld. The devastation wrought by the plague certainly made matters easier for the Marquis of Argyll in that he had no need to carry out the large scale evictions which would otherwise have been a necessary part of his plan to repopulate Kintyre. It had never been a stronghold of the Covenant as the marquis would have liked; so, to achieve for himself the strongest possible political backing, as well as armed support should the need again arise, it was among lowland Covenanting families that he sought the kind of tenants who could not only be relied on politically, but would restore some economic order to his devastated estates.

These newcomers were not themselves farmers, but lairds, or younger sons of lairds, and gentry. In Kintyre, they became tacksmen, that is to say, they were granted, under the system of tack, large areas of land; to these they brought, from their own lowland areas, farmers who would be their sub-tenants, and carry out, with their servants, the actual farming of the land.

These tacks were granted in measures known as 'merklands'. For instance, to the first and most important of his new settlers, William Ralston of that ilk, who already possessed estates in Ayrshire, the marquis granted a tack of 23½ merklands of the former Saddell Abbey lands, with Saddell Castle as his residence. This must have been a very considerable estate indeed, since one merkland was that amount of land assessed at an annual value of 1 merk, or 13s 4d—that being 8oz of silver, the weight required to coin 160 silver Scots pence. The actual area of the merkland was never constant, but expanded or shrank according to the quality of the land. Yet since even a pennyland was a worthy holding, a merkland, at 160 times greater value, would be a very considerable area. It was not until late in the eighteenth century that the then Duke of Argyll had his Kintyre estates measured in acres, from which time the merkland standard passed out of use. Perhaps the largest tack of land granted by the marquis in furtherance of his repopulation scheme was that of 53 merklands to one of his own clan, Dougald Campbell of Inverawe. A Campbell infiltration being an important part of the scheme, Inverawe was given 53 merklands of the estates of Largie, forfeited by that MacDonald laird for his adherence to the royalist cause and his active support of Colkitto. Unfortunately for Inverawe, a fickle parliament restored his lost estates to Largie in 1661—the marquis falling out of favour to the extent of being executed in that same year.

With the plantations came names—apart from Ralston—such as Cunningham, Hamilton, Forbes, Montgomerie, Wallace and Colville—with a preponderance of Campbells from the landward areas of Argyll. The tack system gave to these incomers not a grant or charter but simply a lease, usually of nineteen years. For each merkland of tack, the average rent payable to Argyll was £32 Scots, the tacksmen in their turn receiving from their sub-tenants payment in beast, produce or labour, since the working farmer handled little if any money in the earlier days.

There is little doubt that these newcomers were viewed with suspicion and even hatred by the native Gaels, for as long as perhaps two hundred years. There is just as little doubt, however, that the immigrants, being peaceable, hard-headed, sober and industrious people, laid the foundations of the high-geared agricultural industry that was to grow in Kintyre. The descendants of many of those immigrants are now prosperous, land-owning farmers in Kintyre, long ago fully integrated and, indeed, as proud as any natives of the peninsula who can trace descent back to the sons of Somerled.

While the seventeenth-century infusion of lowland farming blood was a big step forward, it was John, the 5th Duke of Argyll—he assumed the title in 1770 and held it till his death in 1806—who laid the foundations of today's modern farming methods. He abolished the ancient uneconomic method of run-rig culture, and ordered the erection of new large stead-

69

ings, as well as march or boundary dykes of dry stone and turf, and unheard-of shelter belts of trees.

Modern agriculture

As might be expected, those forward-looking methods were not popular with everyone. Old men foresaw the day when the larger farm units being formed would lead to fewer families being supported by the land. The figures on population change (see page 66) may show that their fears were not entirely groundless, since these indicate a large measure of emigration from the best agricultural areas, mostly from 1831 over the following twenty years. This resulted in deserted crofts and smaller farms which were not re-let as they stood but had their acreage lumped together to form larger farms—many of those forming today's very large farms.

Then, in 1955, the pressure of tax demands forced the family of Argyll to dispose by sale of the vast Kintyre estates, mostly consisting of tenanted farms. Overnight, the former tenants became lairds in their own right; practically all of them have, since then, carried out needed improvements to buildings, and to land and stock also.

The methods used are the most modern to be found anywhere in Scotland, the broad acres of south and west being especially suited to the employment of the most complicated tractor-drawn machinery, from the multiple plough to the astonishing potato harvester. The latter not only lifts and gathers this widely grown crop, but disposes of stones and packs the tubers into sacks, which it then sews up neatly ready for transport to markets up and down the country. The warmly productive sandy soil of the west side particularly has of more recent times been found suitable for the production of potatoes for the very earliest markets, and the area rivals neighbouring Ayrshire in this section of the industry.

As might be expected, tillage acreage varies very widely from north and east to south and west. To give one example only,

Page 71 The famous Davaar Isle cave painting

Page 72 The art of carved stones is well represented throughout Kintyre. These are amongst the finest of several collected within the Largie vault in Killean churchyard, near Tayinloan on the west coast

the united parish of Saddell and Skipness, which has an area of over 73 square miles, has a tillage acreage of roughly 524. The parish of Southend, on the other hand, measuring just above 48 square miles, yet has a tillage acreage of about 2,720—or just on five times more than a north-eastern area greater in size by 25 square miles.

Throughout the whole of the peninsula, agriculture may be said to be based largely on pasture. This may seem incredible to the passer-by who views the wide cultivated areas of west and south; yet the fact remains that Kintyre's overall sheep and dairy cattle density is very much above average, while still justly claiming, in the south and west, the highest tillage acreage in the county.

Oats form the main crop, away from the few concentrated potato areas of the sandy west side, the oats being succeeded by turnips and mangolds which, like the oats, go to the winter feeding of stock. Another crop of oats generally follows the roots, after which the rotation takes the form of three to four years under grass.

The high standard of mechanisation on the farms naturally results in the employment of fewer men and women than was the case even as recently as forty years ago, hand milkers in particular having disappeared entirely from the agricultural scene. But recent falling population figures owe very much more to smaller families than to fewer parents; and, since the numbers employed in farming levelled out fairly soon after World War II, these may be expected to remain stable for some time to come.

FISHING

From ancient times a staple industry in the peninsula, herring fishing reached the peak of its productive prosperity during the second half of the eighteenth century, when the vast bulk of all catches were cured and shipped to the West Indies by locally owned vessels as food for the negro slaves.

E

When, soon after the abolition of slavery in 1807, this market diminished and finally closed, the local fish barons—prosperous merchants who had owned and controlled the herring 'busses'—sought new fields of capital investment and turned their attentions to the business of distilling. The fishing industry was thus left to be pursued by working fishermen, the direct forebears of those who have prosecuted it with a fair measure of success ever since.

Up till 1838 only drift nets were used, this being then the only known method of herring fishing. In that year, however, two Tarbert boats conceived the idea of encircling a large shoal which they had discovered in Loch Fyne. Their skippers had unwittingly invented the trawl, or ring net method of securing large catches.

So successful did the new method prove when tried out by others that the use of it spread not only to Carradale and Campbeltown but throughout the country. For some reason, the ring net method was bitterly opposed in certain quarters; its use was banned by legislation, and naval gunboats were sent to fishing waters to enforce the ban. In the ensuing war, much gear was seized and destroyed, and at least one fisherman fatally injured by the action of one gunboat, before the use of the ring net was declared legal in 1867.

Today, just over a century later, herring fishing remains an important Kintyre industry. With modern boats and equipment large catches are still obtained, but a much smaller fleet and far fewer men are employed.

From Campbeltown itself, none of the twenty-three boats engaged in fishing pursues any longer the silver shoals that brought wealth to the town. These vessels are so completely taken up in the presently more lucrative harvest of prawns that it might be difficult, if a change in the market were to occur, to find a skilled herring fishing crew in the port. The number of men presently employed in the fishing industry there had fallen, by late 1972, to eighty-two.

At Carradale, where herring fishing is still prosecuted, sixteen boats give seagoing employment to eighty men; while at Tarbert ninety men man a fleet of twenty-four boats.

DISTILLING

Following the abolition of slavery in 1807 and the loss of the West Indian markets, the herring barons, as has been said, turned their attentions to the distilling trade, thus giving rise to what was to become one of Kintyre's largest and busiest industries.

Aqua-vitae—water of life—was the less civilised forerunner of the *Uisge Beatha*; it seems to have been distilled in Kintyre from at least the early seventeenth century, and probably much earlier. It will never be known now who first gave the product its Gaelic form *Uisge Beatha* or what non-Gaelic Lowlander or Englishman, struggling with the awkward pronunciation of *uisge* came up with something that sounded more like 'whisky'— at which the polite Highlanders, not wishing to laugh, seized on a new word which has since become one of the most famous in any language.

When the burgesses of the growing town of Lochhead jointly rented the nearby farm of Crosshill in 1636, their annual payment was fixed at six quarts of aqua-vitae, which was probably distilled locally. It is known that for long before that time, malt was being produced from oats and barley on farms all over Kintyre; this malt was, however, used almost exclusively for the brewing of ale. Ale, largely farm-brewed, was as much a household beverage then as tea is today, though brewing never became a major industry in the peninsula. At Carskey and at Machrimore, professional brewing was engaged in, on a rather small scale, in the early eighteenth century; and later in that century the firm of Orr Ballantine & Co had a fairly large brewery near to where the present Millknowe indicates the site of the then town mill. There was, about the same time, another,

75

smaller brewery in Bolgam Street. This industry was carried on for only about fifty years.

The distilling of aqua-vitae, as the resultant spirit was still called in the eighteenth century, was almost certainly carried out on most farms—perfectly legally, since there was no duty payable. Very likely professional distillers were also at work from earliest times, though not until 1706 do the minutes of the town council of Campbeltown come up with a mention of 'distillers in the burgh'.

Liquid Gold

From about then on, the business of distilling spirit shows a steady increase; in 1713, inspectors were appointed for the first time, to ensure that spirits for sale were of the required strength and not 'watered down' for quick profit. Seven years later, whisky distilling must have been on the scale of an emerging industry, since, in that year, an enactment signed by fifty local merchants bound them against the handling of any brandy or spirits not produced within the United Kingdom, for a period of three years, since such imports were a severe restriction on the distribution of Campbeltown's own product.

It was still a growing industry when the disastrous harvests of 1782 and 1783 brought the near famine conditions which forced the Commissioners of Supply to take the drastic step of utterly prohibiting the making of whisky, so that the barley might be diverted to the feeding of the almost starving populace. All private stills throughout the county were at the same time temporarily confiscated—their permitted size having already been reduced from ten gallons to two gallons in content. Twelve years later, the government was forced, again by reason of crop failure, to order a two-year suspension of distilling.

While these events must have been a set-back to what was an expanding industry, further difficulties lay ahead in the complicated licensing system adopted by the government. Where, formerly, duty was payable on a presumed number of gallons obtained from a known quantity of wash, the authorities now decided to base the duty on each gallon content of the still —at the same time raising the maximum size of permitted still from 20 to 30 and eventually to 40 gallons. This led to abuses in the matter of still construction which made collection of the estimated revenue difficult and resulted in a compensating increase in the rate of duty—the figure of £9 per gallon being reached for the Highland district in 1797.

The effect of this crippling duty—as far as Kintyre was concerned—was to drive the distilling business underground. For twenty years after the imposition of the tax, not one pint of whisky was distilled legally in Kintyre, though it is known that more than ever before was actually being produced free of any tax and that, apart from illicit distilling, smuggling was engaged in on a large scale.

So rife was this untaxable traffic in spirit that the government passed a law, in 1814, making it illegal for anyone in the Highland area to use a still of a capacity under 500 gallons. This measure not having the desired result, the next move was to abolish the duty on stills—which had started all the trouble—and to replace it with a tax at the high rate of 9s 4½d per gallon of whisky.

This measure met with perhaps cautious approval, but was sufficient encouragement for Messrs John Beith & Company to build in 1817, at the head of Longrow, in Campbeltown, the first large-scale modern distillery. This venture, which was to have a century of success, had for its first six years to compete with the almost unconcealed illicit production of whisky. In 1823, the government took the sensible step of slashing the duty on spirit to 2s 4d per gallon; this measure very soon brought on almost a rush of large-scale legal distillation, against which, combined with the new low rate of duty, the illicit distillers found it no longer profitable to operate.

Within the boundaries of Campbeltown burgh alone, large and well-equipped distilleries sprang up in mushroom fashion from this date. They bore such names as Kinloch, Dalaruan, Hazelburn, Rieclachan, Glenramskill, Kintyre, Dalintober, Scotia, Springbank, Glenside and Albyn—to list only a few of the thirty-four established between 1817 and 1880. Production of whisky in the prospering burgh rocketed from a mere 20,000 gallons in the opening year of the century to an all-time peak of 1,810,226 gallons in 1897.

From that dizzy summit began the slow, but accelerating decline which leaves only two distilleries, Springbank and Glen Scotia, operating today. This shrinkage stemmed from causes less easy to foresee then than to understand now. The rush of new distilleries throughout the Highlands, coupled with speculative buying of large quantities of the product by merchants whose aim was to store for future sale, created first an artificial demand, followed by the inevitable glut that meant a drastic cut-back in production. In Campbeltown alone, only three years after that bumper output, production had been trimmed by considerably more than half a million gallons. The problem of storage began to make itself felt. Where, at one time, sales had been so rapid that no interim warehouse was needed, distillers now required large premises where the whisky could be stored for several years until a purchaser was found. Naturally those distilleries least abundant in the matter of financial backing were the first to go to the wall. Others, struggling through to World War I, were glad enough to be taken over by larger concerns outside the county, which naturally closed down those they were able to make redundant, in order to keep their other works fully operational. Many of these distillery sites have since been demolished to make way for expanding municipal housing—among them the once famous Kinloch, Dalintober, Dalaruan, Glenside and Albyn. Others were converted to, and still serve as, workshops, garages, general stores, and, most notably, the creamery which stands as one of Kintyre's major industries today. A few of the largest old distillery warehouses still serve as storage for maturing whiskies produced elsewhere in Scotland.

If the decline of Kintyre's whisky glory seems a sad one, only the undeniable fact that it was hastened, in the days of high demand, by the production of inferior quality whisky can make it sadder. Springbank, still in the control of the Mitchell family who founded it in 1823, is the one and only distillery to have been in continuous operation since then. Glen Scotia—the one-time Scotia, reopened in 1933 after a five-year closure—stands close to the spot where, in AD 503, Fergus the son of Erc held his first parliament.

COAL MINING

The winning of coal in the south of Kintyre was partly an industry necessarily parallel with others, particularly distilling; yet the most prosperous days of the now vanished coal-mining era were those which followed the collapse of the big whisky boom.

Although peat was traditionally the fire provider throughout the peninsula, the existence of coal on that carboniferous strata running from Fife across to Northern Ireland was probably known even before King James IV of Scotland, in March of 1498, sent an expert, described in the treasurer's accounts as 'a coll man to pas in Kintyr to vesy gif colys may be wonnyn thare'; his name was John Davison.

Since the coal which Davison undoubtedly confirmed as being in plentiful supply was probably required only in such quantities as would fulfil the needs of the royal castles at Tarbert, Kilkerran and Dunaverty, nothing more is heard of it till about 1670, when the baptismal register mentions 'coal carrier' as a parent's occupation. At that time, the site of the coal mining was near the farm of Ballygreggan, where work on a small scale may have been pursued for about a hundred years before a newcomer to the area, Charles MacDowall of Cricken, sought a new and probably more accessible source of supply near West Drumlemble Farm. From here, horse-drawn vehicles conveyed the coal over the then comparatively roadless stretch to Campbeltown where the early distilleries provided its main market.

79

Soon, however, MacDowall saw the need for speedier, smoother transport, and called in the famous engineer James Watt, who surveyed for him the line of a canal, running easily without locks over the three miles of flat land from the mill dam near the colliery into the town at the site where the modern gasworks was to be erected—those works possibly being sited there from the very fact that the coal terminus was close by.

Opening in 1794, the canal's short length was plied by two barges carrying daily the equivalent of forty cart loads into town, where the coal found ready sale at 7s 10½d per ton. By 1875, however, when ownership of the colliery changed hands, the canal was found to be so overgrown with thick weed as to be unnavigable, and the new owners decided to abandon it for a light railway. This improved form of haulage boosted coal output to such an extent that by the end of the first decade of the twentieth century, in addition to keeping distilleries and households well supplied, the Drumlemble pit had built up a small export trade, and was shipping, mostly to Ireland, a surplus roughly four times in excess of MacDowall's entire production of 4,500 tons, achieved a century earlier. Meantime newer improved sources were being opened, so that, by the time the Trodigal pit was in operation, the annual output had topped 100,000 tons.

From 1929 till 1946, coal mining in Kintyre fell into the doldrums, only to be mightily re-vitalised when, in the latter year, the thoroughly modern Argyll Colliery, near Machrihanish on the very west of the peninsula, was formally opened. By January 1950, the National Coal Board gave employment there to 140 men, with the bright promise of that figure being raised to 500 in the near future and confident predictions of a weekly output in excess of 8,000 tons.

This might have been the happy ending to the tale of coalgetting in Kintyre. But it wasn't. Seventeen years after these optimistic forecasts were widely published, the Argyll Colliery, by then employing 250 men, was closed down as being uneconomic. There is no longer a coal industry in Kintyre. But there is still coal, though it has never been of high quality. It may be seen in loose outcrops on the very surface in the glen of Tirfergus—the Land of Fergus, son of Erc, who presumably never discovered a use for any of it.

SALTMAKING

In 1678, the same year that the farm of Ballygreggan became the scene of Kintyre's early coal industry, the business of salt-making was being carried on at Knockhantymore, another farm nearer to what is now the village of Machrihanish on the west coast. Little is recorded of this industry, but it has left its impression; although saltmaking ceased altogether about 1774, local people to this day never speak about going to Machrihanish, they go to 'the Pans'. These are the saltpans, of which very sketchy remains in the form of ancient masonry may still be pointed out near the modern council houses, the main original pans being long buried by sand and gravel on the foreshore, between the now disused lifeboat station and the rocky promontory known as the Big Scone.

The salt—a highly priced commodity—was made from the evaporation of sea water. That the industry was carried on in conjunction with the coal mining seems clear from the fact that both the coal land and the two acres at Knockhanty set aside for saltmaking were the joint tenancy then of John Campbell, chamberlain in Kintyre to the Earl of Argyll, and Alexander Forrester of Knockrioch.

It can only be conjectured that cheaper importation was what brought the salt panning to a close after about a century. But no attempt was subsequently made to revive it.

SHIPBUILDING

From its sea-girt position, it was only natural that Kintyre should turn to the building of ships as one of its industries.

81

At the Tarbert end of the peninsula, the famous yard of Messrs A. M. Dickie turned out yachts and small craft for the greater part of a century before it closed down in 1967; it reopened a few years later on a less ambitious but yearly growing scale.

Down the ages, naval, merchant and fishing vessels were probably built and launched both here and at Campbeltown; of this, though persistent tenuous tradition lingers, no records of any sort have been preserved. It is, however, firmly established that, from about 1700 on, a fairly busy yard which built and repaired seagoing ships was in operation at a site in the royal burgh, near to where the Christian Institute now stands. The ending of the Napoleonic Wars may have started the decline of this industry which disappeared completely in the later 1830s.

Forty years later, a native of the town, named Archibald MacEachern, who had built up a vast fortune trading in Africa, returned to settle in Campbeltown, and was at once struck by the lack of skilled employment among the younger men. His scheme—financed entirely by himself—to set up a shipbuilding yard near the town was an act of philanthropy that was to grow into a thriving industry. As the site for his yard he chose that point known as the Trench, from the earthwork defences established there by the Marquis of Argyll in the seventeenth century. He brought in machinery and built furnaces and a tall chimney stack, at the same time going ahead with the construction of the first vessel to be launched there, a timber schooner of 100 tons gross. This ship, incidentally, had a short, but successful career in the Atlantic trade, before being lost with all hands six years after her launching, in a storm which drove her on to the rocks of Pladda, very close to her native shores.

For a period of forty-five years thereafter, the Campbeltown shipbuilding company prospered, turning out small coasting steamers to begin with, before expanding into the foreign markets with much larger ships—the *Roquelle* of 4,363 gross tons being the biggest ship built at the Trench. That was in

1918. The war ended soon, bringing about a world slump in shipbuilding. The *Akenside*, then on the stocks, was completed and launched in 1922. But, for once, the launching was attended by no celebration. For everyone knew the yard was to close, leaving nearly three hundred men without work.

For nearly half a century the shipyard at Trench Point mouldered and rusted; then, in 1969, it was reopened—in a very small way. The new venture has met with almost instant success; for, at the time of writing, with the new Campbeltown shipyard in operation for only three years, the present work force of something over seventy has good reason for celebration in the shape of a £250,000 order for two seine net trawlers for the north-east. Prospects there are bright indeed.

TRADITIONAL INDUSTRIES

Parallel with ship and boat building, the making of sails and nets has for long been one of Kintyre's traditional industries. At Tarbert, the family sailmaking business of Andrew Lietch has operated a busy loft for three generations. Once fully occupied with the supply of sails for the fishing luggers, the trade today is exclusively pleasure and racing rigs, and sails from the Tarbert loft go to every corner of the globe.

Nets were, in the beginning, woven by the fishermen and their wives by hand. Then, early in the nineteenth century, a factory set up in Bolgam Street in Campbeltown worked the first hand-operated netting looms, using a new method which revolutionised the old. Before the end of that century, engines, notably steam, were being used to drive some of the looms—though certain of the ancient hand looms of as early a date as 1868 are still preserved in working order. In the mid 1920s, the old-established netting firm of Joseph Gundry & Co moved from Bridport in Dorsetshire to take over the Campbeltown Net Works.

With the latest machinery installed, a much increased work

force is now engaged round the clock, not only in the making of herring drift and ring nets for the home market, but in the production of fishing as well as camouflage netting for markets overseas.

Hand-loom weaving was widely carried on at one time, both in the town and all over Kintyre, decreasing in output to almost nothing by 1850, when the introduction of powered machinery brought this industry as well as wool spinning virtually to an end.

The making of linen from home-grown flax was another small industry, commemorated now only in the place-names of Lintmill and Bleachfield not far from the Pans.

Tanning of leather was carried out on a slightly larger scale, there being records of at least two tanworks in the royal burgh. One of these, sited in Lady Mary Row, closed only in 1870; the other, with premises at what is now Tangy Place, went out of business twenty-four years earlier.

Yet another industry which prospered during the first half of the nineteenth century was the once famed iron and brass foundry of Nathaniel McNair & Sons. This enterprising firm were also timber merchants and owned a ship named the *Gleaner* which carried emigrants from Campbeltown to the Americas, returning with loads of timber to be used in shipbuilding. In their foundry in the town they cast the iron street lamps brought into use with the introduction of gas lighting in 1830.

6   COMMUNICATIONS

IN days gone by, any invading army which was not sea-
borne must have found it difficult to get into Kintyre. For
infantry or cavalry there was but the one access, the narrow
isthmus, no wider a thousand years ago than now, from sea to
sea. Traders between the Clyde area and the Inner Isles, rightly
respecting the awesome Mull, used a system of porterage here
since ever trade began. The more prosperous merchants mostly
maintained two vessels, one on Loch Fyne and one at West
Loch Tarbert, employing a string of men and horses to transfer
their goods quickly the few hundreds of yards between the
ships. Traders in a smaller way of business simply had their
much lighter craft dragged, fully laden, from sea to sea, by
teams of horses, first on wooden rollers, graduating to 'slipes'
or sledges; and, by the end of the eighteenth century, to long
low-wheeled vehicles of rude construction.

There was nothing really unusual in this procedure. Such
portages were common in the West Highlands, as the very name
Tarbert—Gaelic *Tarruinn*, drag, *bata*, a boat—implies. The
name occurs fairly frequently throughout Argyll itself, always
pointing to a narrow neck of land between seas.

CANAL PROJECTS

It would be surprising, then, if men did not toy with the idea
of cutting a ditch—a canal, in fact—at this point. Many men
did. A group of these went so far, in 1770, as to ask the engineer
James Watt to make a survey of the project. The report he

made was favourable, but for some reason no action was taken on it for another sixty years, by which time Thomas Telford was busy on the Ardrishaig-Crinan cutting, a distance of ten lock-bedevilled miles.

Henry Bell, of *Comet* fame, was retained to supply an estimate of cost for the Tarbert Canal. His plan was for a straight cut of a mere 1,630yd—no locks, no nonsense. Fifteen years later, a company formed to carry out the project, with a capital of £150,000, secured the approval of parliament to go ahead. Pretty soon, however, the state decided to take control of the project from this company, which dissolved three years later, with the canal not even started. Finally, as recently as 1882, with the Crinan Canal in full swing, the plan for a cut at Tarbert was again discussed seriously. With a proposed width of 75ft and a depth of 20ft, this canal would have taken vessels impossible to handle at Crinan. The capital sum required was £180,000. Government approval was again secured, and the annual profit was worked out at a likely £12,000—a figure, incidentally, very close to the annual *loss* currently being incurred by the Crinan Canal.

The fact that the Tarbert Canal, a dream of more than two centuries, never became a reality, stemmed from a number of causes. Firstly, there was within the government, then as now, much interdepartmental bungling which led to delay in getting the actual spadework started. There were also apparently well-founded fears that such a canal would not be usable at all states of the tide. It would not—as on the Ardrishaig-Crinan route—have the advantage of being overlooked by easily releasable natural reservoirs; while, with a straight sea-to-sea cut, this may not seem of great importance from a practical point, season of low tide might have made such extra supply necessary. In addition, there were fears as to the practicability of keeping the passage clear of such silt as would inevitably, in the frequent stormy conditions, surge in from the West Loch.

Other writers may advance other theories, but the fact remains that the project—which many still declare *would* have been perfectly feasible—never got off the paper it was pictured on.

The shipping firm of David MacBrayne, whose red-funnelled sun was long ere this high in the west, was by no means dismayed. Following the custom of their merchandising predecessors, MacBrayne's maintained a vessel at each side of the isthmus. Travellers from Glasgow to the Inner Isles disembarked daily at Tarbert, and had only a very short portage by coach across the isthmus to where the other steamer waited. On their way, they were likely to meet passengers from Islay and Jura bound for the Clyde. These always had a rather more leisurely time in Tarbert, since they had no need to go aboard till the Clyde-bound ship returned to the pier from its daily call at Ardrishaig.

This daily sailing from the Clyde, by way of the Kyles of Bute to Ardrishaig, was part of the famed 'Royal Route' inaugurated by Queen Victoria in 1847, when she visited the West Highlands by sailing through the Crinan Canal from Ardrishaig to Crinan where the more suitably appointed royal yacht awaited her. Incidentally, 'we found the journey tedious' —a sentiment not shared by a party of her descendants who, more recently, followed the same route in the famous *Bloodhound*.

While it was still a part of MacBrayne's service in the west, the 'Royal Route' was plied by many famous steamers, but none more loved than the swift, sharp-prowed *Columba* built for the company in 1878 by J. & G. Thomson of Clydebank. In her youth, her great paddles drove her through the water at the almost incredible speed of 21 knots; even in graceful old age the *Columba*'s 18 knots was fast enough to outstrip many of her brand new rivals. For most of a lifetime, this grand old ship—which actually had a post office on board—carried her complement of up to 2,000 passengers, as well as mail, from the Clyde to Ardrishaig and ports between. It was, in the end, the transference of mail carriage from sea routes to the faster roads of the 1960s that led to the historic steamer service by the Kyles of Bute to Tarbert and Ardrishaig being discontinued. Today, only one steamer calls at Tarbert, on one day per week during the summer, a season which ends by decree on the second Saturday of September. This is the dignified *Waverley*, the last sea-going paddle steamer still operating anywhere in the world.

This vessel, owned by the Caledonian Steam Packet Co— now Caledonian MacBrayne Ltd—attracts many visitors who see her as the surviving member of a well-loved race of Clyde steamer. Her open engine room, with gigantic gleaming connecting rods turning the paddles, her shining pistons gliding like silk along their guides, magnetises boys of eight to eighty and holds them spellbound. Though built as lately as 1947, to replace the original *Waverley*, lost at Dunkirk, this dignified vessel is no imitation in any sense of the word. Available for charter, she is very much in demand by societies of ship enthusiasts everywhere.

The daily service from the West Loch to Islay, Jura and Gigha is still maintained. The emphasis is, naturally, on commerce, and few passengers are carried, save in the summer season when tourists throng to see those isles. The motor vessel *Arran*, at present engaged on this run, is one of MacBrayne's increasing fleet of car ferries, in very great demand by the many who, loudly declaiming their love of remote areas, are reluctant to be parted from their cars.

As with Tarbert there is nowadays no steamer link between Campbeltown and the Clyde, other than the summertime excursions which are still extremely popular. Road and air transport have between them relegated to fond memory the last two gallant, graceful, tall-funnelled old ships, *Davaar* and *Dalriada*, with which the Campbeltown & Glasgow Steam Packet Joint Stock Co Ltd provided the main link between

Page 89 (*right*) The unique war memorial at Skipness village; (*below*) the famous Campbeltown Cross, which, having stood outside the Town House in the Main Street since the early seventeenth century, was taken down for safety during the bombing of World War II, and afterwards re-erected in its original position fronting the harbour

Page 90 Campbel-
town, Main Street,
running from the
harbour upwards to
Castlehill where, in
1609, Argyll built his
famous castle of which
no trace remains. The
prominent spire is that
of the Town Hall

Kintyre and the outside world from the 1880s to the early 1930s. The *Davaar*, built for this special service in 1885, was for long after her natural day a delight to ship-lovers, with her beautifully formed 'clipper' bow and her tall funnel. The *Dalriada*, launched in 1926 and capable of 18 knots, was regarded as being one of the fastest single-screw steamers of her day. Her launching, incidentally, marked an important anniversary for the operating company, which had up till then maintained an unbroken record of steamship service in these waters for just a hundred years.

These fine old ships sailed from Campbeltown for the Clyde on alternate days, with calls at Carradale, Lochranza, Gourock and Greenock. Since one was always on the homeward trip as the other was outward bound, their schedule did not allow the day tripper a few hours either in Glasgow from Campbeltown, or in Campbeltown from Glasgow.

The 'day trip' was to develop from a quietly new form of family recreation into one of the Clyde Coast's major industries. It began—as far as Campbeltown is concerned—with the launching in 1901, from Denny's yard in Dumbarton, of the world's first turbine propelled merchant ship. This revolutionary vessel, named *King Edward*, was constructed within a few months to the order of her managing owner, John Williamson, the engines being supplied and fitted by Parsons Marine Steam Turbine Company.

Not only was 1901 the year of the great Glasgow Exhibition, it was also the hottest summer for many years before and since. Put into service on the newly founded day trip to Campbeltown, the new fast ship often had to leave behind scores of disappointed late-comers—even on the frequent occasions when she carried many more than the number laid down as her capacity.

Many other turbine steamers, from the probable favourite *Queen Alexandra* down to the present *Queen Mary II*, followed *King Edward* on what is still probably the most popular day trip from the Clyde.

F

The need for a type of drive-on drive-off vessel capable of carrying not only touring cars but container lorries gave rise, during the 1960s, to an enterprise known as Western Ferries, which has become Kintyre's most revolutionary communications change of the century. A few miles south of Tarbert, where the West Loch scythes between Kilberry and Kintyre, there was, until recently, a tiny cormorant-haunted tidal islet known as *ceann na creig*—end of the rock. This is still a fair enough description of a place which, today—at the smooth end of a concrete causeway, its rock hidden by terminal offices, parking space and wide landing berth—has become anglicised into 'Kennacraig'.

From here the red and white *Sound of Jura*, built by Norwegians with centuries of experience in just the kind of freight problems which beset these isles, makes three daily runs to Islay. From Port Askaig, its terminal there, *Sound of Gigha*, a smaller vessel of the landing-craft type shuttles back and forth between Islay and Jura. The service will take in Gigha also, if plans at present in hand for a suitable terminal on that isle ever take concrete shape. An earlier attempt to establish such a service for Gigha regrettably failed when, in January 1972, the jetty, which could be used only in rarely favourable conditions, was carried away by a storm. These are inhospitable seas, especially in winter; yet it is a rare occurrence for the *Sound of Jura* to miss a crossing, whether with a few cars, vans or tractors, or loaded from stem to stern with immense containers. It is probable that Gigha also will benefit from the carrier service offered by Western Ferries, which, entering the lists only a few years ago as a small private enterprise, was in 1972 able to fight off a take-over bid by the Scottish Transport Group.

At the other end of the peninsula, from the main port of Campbeltown, the same company operates *Sound of Islay* on a similar service to and from Red Bay in Cushendall—at present the shortest ferry between Scotland and Northern Ireland. At first expected to operate—with necessary restrictions in winter—throughout the year, this service has settled to the form of a daily return trip on Mondays, Fridays, Saturdays and Sundays, from 15 to 30 June and from 1 to 17 September. During July and August the vessel makes a double run on each of these days, as well as one return trip on Tuesdays, Wednesdays and Thursdays.

Clearly, the car ferry is opening Kintyre to the rest of Scotland. From a point on the west side, midway between Kennacraig and the village of Whitehouse, a five-mile stretch of single-track road crosses over to Kilbrannan Sound in the east. As it rises to the spine of the peninsula, the mountains of Arran, startlingly near, are viewed to better advantage than from within the isle itself or from any other part of the mainland of Scotland. By narrow, twisted, ancient humpbacked bridges, this road drops right to the sandy shore at Claonaig, where Kintyre's very latest line of communication is operated by Caledonian MacBrayne Ltd.

This is the car-ferry service between Lochranza in the north of Arran and Claonaig in Kintyre, which has opened up exciting possibilities. Linked as it is with the Ardrossan-Brodick crossing, no more scenically splendid approach to Kintyre and the Inner Isles could be devised. True, over its first season of operation in 1972, this service had its teething troubles. First and foremost, though operating from different ports, it virtually replaced a large car ferry service which the Caledonian Steam Packet Company had run—unsuccessfully for lack of patronage—during the summer of 1970 up to the end of September 1971, from Fairlie to Tarbert, with a call at Brodick en route. Where such a service had failed it might have seemed unlikely that public demand warranted the opening of an alternative. Landing on the tarry planks of Tarbert pier from a high-decked, hissing and clanking ship, however, in no way compares with driving down a ramp on to the blindingly white sands of Claonaig, following the shortest possible sea crossing. Also, the imagination of the traveller is caught by the possibility of avoiding traffic-bedevilled roads, and finding himself, in a theoretical few hours from leaving, say, Glasgow, actually with the roads of Kintyre beneath his wheels, and another ferry to Islay a matter of minutes away.

In down-to-earth practice, however carefully timetables were studied, such theory did not always work out over the 1972 season of the ferry's operation. The MV *Kilbrannan* was a very small vessel, carrying five cars and fifty passengers, and the Sound whose name she bore is open at the point of crossing to the prevailing south-westerly winds; these were frequently too strong to permit her to sail. From the viewpoint of foot passengers there was also the legitimate grumble that of the eight probable daily crossings into Kintyre, only one connected with a bus.

In the early summer of 1973 the slightly larger vessel, *Rhum*, came into service on this route and, in a not notably calm season, set a good record by losing an average of only two days per month due to bad weather. The popularity of the service is giving rise to speculation as to the possible provision of a vessel able to carry fifteen vehicles.

In the matter of new vessels, Western Ferries are also actively occupied. They have plans to replace the little *Sound of Gigha*, which at present plies between Port Askaig and Feolin in Jura, with a new ship; in this event the *Sound of Gigha* would be put into service between Tarbert and the lower Loch Fyne mainland, with a terminal probably at Portavadie—a new route which would cut out many hours and miles of winding, sealoch-rounding roads.

With old sea links gone to make way for new, one ferry in Kintyre remains unchanged, and, so far as can be foreseen unchangeable, at least in the near future. This is the semi-open motor boat carrying foot passengers only which provides the main link with the pleasant Isle of Gigha. Such ferries as this were, until comparatively recent times, privately operated, landing passengers on piers and jetties which were also privately owned, and seldom the better for that. Nowadays the county council runs the many such ferries needed in a sea-girt area like Argyll. The boats used are strong and seaworthy, the operators—often ex-fishermen—are highly skilled, and grand new concrete jetties replace the often insecure boulder-built landing stages of a generation past.

What no council may do, however, is to legislate for quiet waters. In winter time especially, there are many days when it is at the least unwise for the Gigha ferryman to venture forth. Often, at such times, he has no need to, since no one is anxious to venture along with him anyway.

Then, perchance, someone is taken suddenly ill. A doctor is needed; the nearest one is at the tiny village of Muasdale, a little way down the coast from the ferry terminal at Tayinloan. From information passed to him by telephone, the doctor has to decide whether to cross—by asking the ferryman to come for him—or to instruct the resident nurse to take the patient across right away, while he summons an ambulance to the jetty. The doctor's decision is not swayed by his own desire to avoid a tossing, but from the fear that, should he cross and then find the patient in need of urgent removal to hospital, enough time has been wasted to allow the storm to reach such pitch that neither he, the ferryman nor the patient are able to cross to the Kintyre shore that day—or night.

Since no aeroplane can land on Gigha's rocky fastness, this problem must remain yet awhile with a race of people to whom contending with one difficulty or another has, over the centuries, become a way of life.

ROADS

Road communications into, out of and throughout Kintyre are adequate. A good 'A' class road follows the west coast from

Tarbert for nearly twenty-nine miles to Westport. There, where a three-mile sickle of firm white sand curves its roller-washed way to the village of Machrihanish, the road strikes eastward to Campbeltown.

The single track road which crosses the peninsula about five miles south of Tarbert follows the east shore closely to serve the village of Skipness. At the fork at Claonaig on Kilbrannan Sound, this road turns sharply southward to continue its narrow, often precipitous and corkscrew way along an exceedingly picturesque twenty-nine miles to Campbeltown. Surfaces on both classes of road are maintained at the higher than average standard of which Argyll people are justly proud; and few families are without a car.

There is a twice-daily bus service both ways between Glasgow and Campbeltown and points between. The greater part of this was inherited by Scottish Motor Transport from David Mac-Brayne Ltd in the late 1960s, with connections taken up at Tarbert by the Campbeltown-based West Coast Motor Company, which also co-operates with SMT in conveying foot passengers to Tarbert from the Lochranza-Claonaig ferry. The same firm serves all of the east coast as far north as Skipness with a daily bus in summer, and a thrice-weekly winter service.

The more populated end of the peninsula—from Campbeltown south and westward—has been served with suitable internal transport by the family firm of MacConnachie since the days before the invention of the motor bus. Today, especially in summertime, this firm operates a busy shuttle service to and from Machrihanish, traditionally by far the most popular picnic area for both natives of the town and visitors.

THE WEE TRAIN

The lingering popularity of this somewhat uninspiring village may not be entirely unconnected with tender memories of that one section of Kintyre's internal transport system which was remarkable enough long after its day to warrant its study by both students and experts in the science of locomotion. The Campbeltown & Machrihanish Light Railway was accorded that title only on posters and fare tickets. To Kintyre men, wherever they chanced to foregather, it was 'the wee train'. And to them, it was the only wee train in all the world.

It was in 1773—just about a year before the panning of salt ceased at the place later to be known as Machrihanish—that the engineer James Watt was asked to survey a line for a projected canal, with the object of speeding up the haulage of coal from the pit into Campbeltown. Then, a century or more later, the then new coal company hit on the idea that a narrow-gauge railway might be even better than the canal, which, after all, would not be all that much faster than the horse and cart.

This railway of 2ft 3in gauge, running a distance of just over 4½ miles from Drumlemble pit to the coal depot at the east end of Argyll Street in Campbeltown, opened without fuss on 23 May 1877 and without the remotest hint that it would one day become celebrated in song and story, far from these shores. Coal sold that day in the depot at Campbeltown for 8s per ton.

For railway enthusiasts, other more learned volumes deal minutely with the technicalities of laying such a railway as this was to become—taking into account the problems of gradient, cuttings, bridges, curves and costs. This book concerns itself only with the romantic story of this, the most isolated railroad in the kingdom; and a unique history it was to prove. Up till the opening of the twentieth century, few people in Kintyre even noticed the growing fashion of tourism; perhaps none at all saw in it the birth of an industry that was to surpass distilling and even rival agriculture in the years ahead. Some eyes were opened to its potential when, in 1901, the fast turbine steamer *King Edward* opened the peninsula to a flow of day trippers, which quickly turned to a flood. The horse-drawn carriages which conveyed those trippers on a necessarily brief ride across the peninsula to the surf-beaten shores of the Atlantic at

Machrihanish, had their resources stretched to the utmost. It was an enjoyable outing; the curious little narrow-gauge railway, with its fussing engines hauling coal from the pit into the town, was one of the sights to be seen here and there, from the bumpy road.

Among those who saw it through more than ordinarily penetrating eyes was John Williamson, owner of the *King Edward*, his friend Denny, who had built the steamer, and his other friend, Parsons, who had fitted her turbine engines. Why, they asked one another, should not this railway be extended a little at either end, and its engines put to hauling passenger coaches instead? Machrihanish was not only being developed as a tourist resort; the game of golf was becoming very popular with those who sojourned there.

And so, in 1905, the Campbeltown & Machrihanish Light Railway Co was born. The coal company gladly sold to the newcomers their existing line, complete with locomotive and everything else, for £4,500, and confirmed their belief in the new venture by subscribing for six and a half thousand shares in the company.

First, the line had to be extended. This was a fairly simple matter since there were no stations anywhere—at the Campbeltown end passengers boarded in Hall Street above the Quay, and at the Machrihanish terminal they dismounted in a field near the Ugadale Arms hotel. Some 'halts' were laid down, however, mostly at cross roads. In the event, the train could be halted just about anywhere anybody wanted to get on or off. There were ten level crossings in all, and none had gates—a point of no great importance, since, though the prospectus spoke glowingly of this smooth speedy way of travel, the train never attained more than an average 12½ mph.

The railway opened to passenger traffic on Friday, 17 August 1906. There had been much local opposition to it, on the grounds of noise, danger and dirt. This opposition lasted right up to the day following the opening run, Saturday, when local people jammed every carriage for a run to Machrihanish. From that moment, they took 'the wee train' to their hearts. It was their own; they were fiercely proud of it, and none dare breathe one word of disparagement against it.

The wee train's timetables were very slightly complicated, at first sight. There was the 'ordinary' train and the 'express' non-stop—the latter specifically in connection with the steamers. The 'ordinary' was scheduled to stop, by request, at Plantation, Moss Road, Lintmill, Drumlemble, Machrihanish Farm and Trodigal, which seems an awful lot of stops, even if that were all, in a very short distance. The 'express', on the other hand, did not stop anywhere—which pleased not only the tourist but local commuters also, since they had a secret pact with their wee train that caused it always to accomplish the 'ordinary' and 'express' runs in exactly the same time. And so everyone was happy.

As the railway became an established mode of transport, it was natural that it should be used by secondary pupils from the outlying farm towns, who travelled daily to the grammar school in Campbeltown and joined the train here and there, wherever they chanced to live. A pupil wishing to 'jink' school could do so only by hiding in a ditch, for, should one be in sight the train would wait or even reverse along the line for an unwilling lingerer, whistling urgently the while.

In winter, the regular engines *Atlantic* and *Argyll* would be taken off for extensive servicing, and replaced temporarily by the aged *Chevalier*. This suited the scholars perfectly, since this temperamental veteran often refused to leave its Campbeltown base on cold mornings, or, having left, decided not to make the return run. When it did run willingly, it could be depended on to stick halfway up Narrowfield Brae, with the pupils leaning out and cheering as the train rolled back down, to have a second and often a third try for the summit.

Among the officials and drivers, there seems to have been a fair crop of characters—very notably one driver who was a

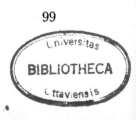

keen contender in the track events at the local games. His favourite method of getting himself fit for these contests was to jump from his cab and run alongside the train for a spell, before swinging back to the controls again. In the close season for athletics, this same driver used to watch out for rabbits along the line. It is alleged that in Dalivaddy Moss there may still be, for the gathering, lumps of coal which he threw mightily and not always in vain. On many occasions, without stopping the train, he would leap from his engine, jump over the fence, collect his kill, and be back at the controls all within seconds.

In spite of this apparently casual method of running a railway, the twenty-five years over which the C & M was operated were marred by only one accident, regrettably with fatal results for an engine cleaner. A thorough inquiry into the cause of the accident, in which the train struck a stationary engine at a speed of only 2 mph, showed it to be the result of a certain irregularity—only one of many which were part and parcel of the happy working of this carefree line.

The temporary closure of the coal pit, from 1929 on, and the depression which blanketed the country in those years were probably among the factors which brought about the decline and final closure, in 1931, of the Campbeltown & Machrihanish Light Railway. With trippers very thin on the ground, the company attempted for a short time to bridge the gap between bad and good times by buying second-hand buses to maintain their service. The local coaching firm of A. & P. MacConnachie had, however, already established a bus service—with better vehicles.

Officially the railway company did not go into liquidation until 1933. But before the steamer *Queen Alexandra* arrived to open the tourist season of 1932, the buses had put the wee train off its tracks for the last time. By June, the whole outfit—rails, wagons, engines etc—had been sold for scrap. The engines were dismantled, broken up and shipped away, and by the next summer the coaches were serving as holiday cabins at Trench Point, where they could be identified for many years afterwards. Today, it is hard to discern where the line ran, without having the cuttings and embankments pointed out here and there.

Though this was the only railway line ever to operate in Kintyre, it was neither the first nor the most ambitious to be projected for the peninsula. In the 1880s a scheme was formulated for the construction of a line from Campbeltown up the easy gradient of the west side to Tarbert, thence by way of Ardrishaig to Inveraray, and on to Dalmally where it would link with the main Oban-Callander line.

The scheme, though it met with more objection than the later light railway did, was well received by the town council of Campbeltown, which was prepared to bless it with financial support. For some reason, however, the project was dropped, before ever a turf had been cut. After such a lapse of time, it is hard to discover just why; but the concensus of inherited opinion points to the then Duke of Argyll as having come down on the side of the objectors to the scheme. Certainly, whatever the duke said went—or, in this case, did not go.

AIR SERVICES

For the traveller in a hurry, or for one who simply wished to enjoy the best possible view of some of the finest scenery in Scotland's west, Kintyre's airport has for many years provided a link with Glasgow, Islay and points beyond. Largely created by nature, the airport lies near the village of Machrihanish, cunningly hidden behind the line of marram-fronted white sand dunes which defy the Atlantic rollers in their efforts to flood the low-lying Laggan of Kintyre—as once undoubtedly they did.

It is a three-mile, ten-minute bus ride from Campbeltown to the airport, which shares a corner of the Laggan with what was described only a few years back as 'a Royal Air Force slum'. Up to the mid-1960s this forgotten bastion of the RAF consisted of an unsightly huddle of dirty flat-roofed brick buildings, many with gaping broken windows staring out on to another unattractive jumble of wartime Nissen huts and flapping corrugated iron sheds. Since then the RAF has given its base at Machrihanish a face-lift in the shape of administration buildings and family living quarters which would serve as a model for any in the country—though few would be likely to enjoy such a perfect setting.

The closely adjacent civil airport, which in earlier days shared the primitive ground facilities, also has its own modern buildings rivalling any in Europe for comfort. British European Airways operates a service which was inaugurated in 1933 as Britain's first internal air passenger route. Glasgow, which lies about 134 road miles away, is only fifteen luxurious flying minutes from take-off at Machrihanish. It was hoped that the daily service from Glasgow, which is of inestimable time-saving value to businessmen, might be supplemented by a summertime evening flight. This would have made it possible for day trippers to come from Glasgow on the morning plane to Machrihanish, which touched down before going on over the sea to Islay and again on the return trip, so that they could spend the best hours of the day either in Kintyre or on Islay before returning to Glasgow on an evening plane. However, in 1973 the Campbeltown-Islay link was discontinued and freight services to Campbeltown from Glasgow withdrawn as part of a rearrangement of schedules and services by BEA on economic grounds. These changes met with bitter opposition from the town council of Campbeltown and local businessmen, who in meetings with BEA officials sought for an improvement in the present service to the airport.

An outstanding and revolutionary supplement to the air services is found in the 'mercy flights' which are frequently undertaken. Doctors in Kintyre turn to this air ambulance with life-saving regularity in cases where patients, often road accident casualties, are in urgent need of the facilities of a city hospital.

7   THE LIFEBOAT SERVICE

JUTTING out, as it does, into the very busy shipping lane from the Clyde coast to the Irish Sea and the wider Atlantic, and with its own rock-bound coasts exposed to the white fury of frequent southerly gales, Kintyre not surprisingly has a long lifeboat tradition.

In Campbeltown, where the modern *City of Glasgow II* rocks to her mooring ropes in a constant state of readiness, a lifeboat station has been maintained without interruption since 1861. The present boat is the successor to a long line of rescue vessels and its crew are heirs to a tradition of selfless valour that is common to all fishing towns and villages round the storm-battered coasts of Britain.

Such a reputation for cruelty was acquired by the reef-studded coast of the Mull that for a time lifeboats were maintained not only at Campbeltown harbour, but at Southend and Machrihanish also. In the days of sail and oars the time saved by having a boat at both these stations could be vital. With the modern high-powered diesel engine, combined with such aids as radar and radio communication, boats and crews operate from Campbeltown only. The other two stations, which had done much valuable rescue work in days gone by, were closed in 1929. At Machrihanish where the former lifeboat shed and launching ways stand as a crumbling monument to many brave deeds, it may easily be observed that the position of a large rock must have made launching a tricky, if not an impossible task at certain states of the tide. This could have been a factor in the decision to close that station, as lifeboats increased in size and draught.

The earliest lifeboat in the records of the Campbeltown station was the *Lord Murray*, delivered in 1861. Between then and 1876, it was launched eight times, and saved thirty-five lives from the raging sea. The *Lord Murray* was, as were all lifeboats of its day, completely dependent on sail and strong arms to its oars. Engine power, radar and radio have now taken the place of oars and the old coxswain's capacity of navigating by 'the smell of the wind'. However, the rule of carrying two pints of rum for restorative purposes, with ginger wine for

Campbeltown lifeboat

teetotallers, has never been changed. A line-throwing pistol has replaced the strong arm of the bowman, the megaphone has become an electronic loud hailer, and cans of self-heating soup have dispensed with the often dangerous task of lighting a stove.

The tradition and system of organisation on a completely voluntary basis have not changed since the Royal National Lifeboat Institution came into being in 1824. In places like Campbeltown, sons have followed fathers into this selfless, highly dangerous service for generations, and for no reason other than that they know that the men out there are seafarers like themselves, contending with the same elements and dependent, when the need arises, on the outstretched hand of a brother.

The *Lord Murray* was followed, in 1876, by the *Princess Louise* which served the station for twelve years before being replaced by the *Mary Adelaide Harrison*. In 1898 the very famous *James Stevens II* entered the service, followed in 1911 by the *Richard Cresswell*, and in 1912 by the *William MacPherson*. From 1929 through the busy sea years of World War II, the first *City of Glasgow* carried out many spectacular rescues, supported by boats on temporary duty, such as the trusty *Duke of Connaught*, of which boat and her crew tales of almost incredible daring will long be told. The *City of Glasgow* was called out on ninety-one occasions during her twenty-four years stay at the Campbeltown station, saving 173 lives. Since 1953, when the modern, splendidly equipped *City of Glasgow II* was delivered to Campbeltown station, the need for such a service on this very treacherous part of the coast has not by any means lessened. In eight years of service she was launched thirty-five times, saving in that period a total of thirty-one lives.

The blackboards in the lifeboat station at Campbeltown maintain briefly-worded records to show that in the first hundred years since the station was established there, successive boats have answered 184 mercy calls, the number of lives saved being 374.

It must be understood that lifeboats go out often, and after many hours of contending with furious seas may return without having been able to save one life. There is also the occasion when a chance flare over a dark sea is suspected of being a call for help. The lifeboat goes out whatever the conditions, and may, in such cases, search for an exhausting round of the clock without finding trace of any vessel in distress. Then there are the other occasions when information is exact, the location clearly pinpointed, and the number of human lives at stake known.

Page 107   (*above*) A carpenter carries out between-tide repairs at Carradale; (*below*) the MacBrayne vessel, *Locheil*, loading at the West Loch for Islay

Page 108 (*left*) The Caledonian Steam Packet paddle steamer *Waverley*—the last ocean-going paddle ship in the world; (*below*) Kennacraig. The Western Ferries roll-on roll-off vessel *Sound of Jura* unloading container traffic from Islay. This fast method of delivery has revolutionised freight services to the Inner Isles

Whatever the nature of the service, whatever the result, the response of the crew is always the same, and the report of the secretary couched in the same simple, unemotional terms.

'JAMES STEVENS II'

Of the old-time oars and sail lifeboats, perhaps the most affectionately recalled is the *James Stevens II*, which over twenty-six launchings saved forty-six lives. Not always did her longest and most dangerous missions produce the most spectacular results. A good example of this kind of service—it is always a 'service', incidentally, never a 'mission'—is provided by the record of one of *James Stevens II*'s exploits early in the present century.

December 28 1908 dawned darkly over Kintyre, with a gale, laced by snow flurries, shrieking out of the south-east. At a quarter to ten o'clock that morning, a telegraph message was handed to Captain Gardiner, who was at that period honorary secretary of the Kintyre branch of RNLI. In passing, it should be explained that all calls are dealt with by the secretary, and it is he, not the coxswain, who calls out the lifeboat—or not, as the case may be. The honorary secretary may be said to be the boss of the lifeboat as long as she is ashore and moored, while once afloat the coxswain's word is law.

The telegraphed message gave news of the *Bessie Arnott*, a schooner of 180 tons which had been driven ashore near Sliddery on the south of Arran and was clearly in urgent need of assistance. Captain Gardiner called out the lifeboat, crewed by fourteen men under coxswain George McEachran. It says a vast deal for their state of preparedness that within twenty-two minutes from the delivery of the message, the *James Stevens* was clear of the slipway and, with sail closely reefed, clawing her way into the mountainous seas that met her as soon as she cleared the harbour.

By 1 pm the lifeboat had manoeuvred close enough to the

G

wreck, where she lay hammering on her beam ends close to the shore, to see that three men clung to her in an exhausted condition—one appeared already dead.

By using the anchor as a stay, the skilled lifeboatmen worked their own craft as close as they dared to the stricken ship; too close in the end, as without warning one gigantic sea picked up the lifeboat and landed her crashingly on top of the doomed vessel, not only damaging the bottom, but causing the bowman to be washed overboard, and two crew members besides the coxswain to be thrown from their places and hurt. Almost before it could be realised that the lifeboat was holed in the bottom, the next wave lifted her clear from the wreck, leaving the bowman clinging for his life to the ship's rigging. It was now plain that the rudder of the lifeboat had also suffered severe damage and control of her was difficult. Nevertheless, with supreme skill, the crippled boat was manoeuvred once more close enough to the wreck for the bowman, who took his chance on the back-wash, to be hauled aboard in a soaked, half-frozen condition.

This and the other injuries to his crew, as well as the damage to the boat, caused the coxswain to try to make the best of his way back to base, no simple task under such conditions, without renewing the attempt to relieve the now completely wrecked vessel.

Such a decision is always a hard and bitter one for any coxswain to have to take; yet he must not be seen to waver for an instant. His crew members are his friends and comrades, toughened seamen like himself; yet a young, less experienced lifeboatman's usefulness as a crew member can depend almost entirely on his confidence in the coxswain, who must therefore shoulder full responsibility for instantaneous decisions.

In this particular instance, Coxswain McEachran's decision and skilled seamanship probably saved the lives of his crew—and, in a few hours, other lives in dire peril. As it was, the return to base was accomplished under conditions dangerous in the extreme. The damage to the rudder made steering so difficult in the mountainous seas that only the use of a sea anchor, or drogue—a sort of conical open-ended canvas bag—allowed them to keep the lifeboat on her fiercely contested course for Campbeltown harbour, where she arrived in the winter darkness at 5 pm. It says a great deal for the quality of these men that only two are recorded as in need of medical attention. The others, after a hot meal, were ready to respond to distress calls which a bare four and a half hours later went up from two vessels stranded and being pounded to pieces on the shore within Campbeltown harbour.

The secretary, Captain Gardiner, took the decision to send the lifeboat out again, damaged as she was—but, this time, with himself as deputy coxswain, since the doctor utterly forbade Coxswain McEachran from going out again that night.

Captain Gardiner asked for a volunteer crew, and found himself with most of those who had already spent the whole furious winter day in vain exhausting effort to help the *Bessie Arnott*—from which vessel, incidentally, one man was later found to have been washed ashore alive. With the crew on board, it was found that the ebbing tide had left the *James Stevens* partly grounded near the pier where she had been moored. But, as so often, in spite of the shrieking fury of the wind and the thickening of the snow, many townspeople had assembled by the pier. The temporary coxswain bawled them into service, passing them a long rope by means of which they were able to drag the lifeboat into a depth sufficient for her to struggle off into the blackness of the December night, in the teeth of a gale that, increasing in fury, sent spindrift flying in high spouts across the loch, where the snow was driving mercilessly on a level with the seas.

The lifeboat made first for the ship seemingly most exposed to the fury of the night; she proved to be a small coasting schooner, the *Jane*, loaded with coal and bound for Larne when struck by the storm. The three men on board, a father and two sons, had lashed themselves to the rigging of their battered vessel before being completely overwhelmed by exposure and exhaustion.

Once again, the lifeboat tried the manoeuvre—one which has saved countless lives—of 'drifting down on the anchor', that is, letting the boat's anchor go, to windward, so that, using it as a stay, the lifeboat may be worked close to the wreck. This time, however, due to the exceeding fury of the surf and the soft bottom at that part of the loch, the anchor failed to hold and the lifeboat was sent spinning past the stricken schooner. Strong arms strained at the oars, in an effort to regain position, but in the teeth of the increasing gale the tiring rescuers were unable to make an inch, and were in danger of being thrown on to a jetty not far from the pier they had left. Once more the townspeople came to their aid. Ropes were thrown, and the lifeboat was dragged into deeper water, her crew straining at the oars in the noisy darkness. Over and over again, the *James Stevens* strove to reach the beached and storm-battered wreck, and over and over again she was driven back by the howling might of the snow-laden gale.

This went on till 1.30 am, by which time the gale had increased in fury. The lifeboatmen, many of whom had been on duty for almost sixteen hours, were soaked through, chilled to the bone, bruised in every muscle and in sore need of rest. It was decided to put in for hot drinks of tea and rum at the pier, with an opportunity for the men to take some food, and change into dry clothing which their families held ready for them.

It was a brief respite. Captain Gardiner called for a crew to pursue the work of rescue. Five of those who stepped forward had already spent all night in the lifeboat, as well as having sustained the earlier, almost disastrous attempt at rescue on the Arran shore. Yet, out they went into the fury of the howling dark, and for five hours more, with sleet and snow colder than the spray that lashed them constantly, they strove over and over again, to reach the helpless men tied fast to the rigging of the *Jane*.

At the end of that time, close to 7.30 am, a miraculous lull in the gale allowed the lifeboat to be worked close enough to the wreck for the three storm-battered men to be cut down from the rigging. One, the father, was already dead from exposure, but the sons were both alive! At this moment, voluntary aid appeared in the shape of another boat which, in the lull, had bravely come out to help the lifeboatmen. To this boat the rescued men were transferred, for a quick run to safety, while the *James Stevens II*, her full task not yet accomplished, turned to the other victim of that night's fury, the ketch *Margaret Wotherspoon*, and with less difficulty now, took her crew of three men aboard. Then, bending aching and bruised backs to the big oars, the lifeboatmen strained to reach their base, which they did by 8.30 am. Still valiantly pulling were men who had just completed nearly twenty-three hours of relentless toil, almost without respite, in the most hazardous and comfortless conditions it is possible to imagine. Bruised and cut, and utterly spent, they were sent home to get the rest they needed so badly. The others, including Captain Gardiner, stayed on to make temporary, quick repairs to the broken lifeboat—which was as ready as they could make her when, the very next night, she was called out on yet another mission of mercy.

Boats have, of course, been vastly improved since 1908. But the strength of the lifeboat is measured, now as then, by the quality of her crew, and most especially of the coxswain, who has to be a man of almost indestructible toughness, admitting of no defeat, mentally alert, icily decisive and possessed of much of the relentless driving force and endurance of the elements he undertakes to fight. In addition, even in these days of radio and radar, he has to have an indefinable sort of instinct, the quality which, perhaps above all, keeps him one jump ahead of the tempest and tides with which he contends.

COXSWAIN DUNCAN NEWLANDS

Such a man was Duncan Newlands, the almost legendary coxswain of Campbeltown lifeboat for eighteen years; when he retired in 1962, he had been a crew member for forty-one years. Over that period he had gone out on a hundred services, playing his part in the saving of something over three hundred human lives. His exploits and those of the brave men who accompanied him, would fill a large book. For the purposes of this short account, a few typical examples may be selected.

On 29 January 1945, a time of year when it is usual for all the fury of the seas driving from the world's end to concentrate on the Mull of Kintyre, a gale out of the south had been increasing in force all day. So severe was it that the naval authorities—it was still wartime, with the Royal Navy in command—issued an order closing the harbour to all shipping.

By 6.55 pm, when the telephone rang in the house of Anthony McGrory, the honorary secretary of the RNLI, the gale was gusting to force 9 and the night as black as pitch. The message informed him of red distress flares having been seen off the south end of Arran and thought to be from a naval trawler *Dunraven Castle*, with a complement of twenty-five officers and men. Because of the order closing the harbour, McGrory had to go, as fast as walking would take him, to the naval command, to point out that such an order must not—and, as far as he was concerned, would not—apply to the lifeboat. His argument won, he now had to enlist help in going from door to door in the wild dark, calling out the lifeboat crew. Again, it seems remarkable that under all those delaying difficulties of wartime, the *City of Glasgow* was manned and on her way just fifty-five minutes from the moment the phone had shrilled in McGrory's house.

The *City of Glasgow* was a very up-to-date 52ft Barnett type boat, fitted with buoyant air cases and watertight compartments, and could be expected to take a pounding in shallow waters and still remain afloat. The main problem facing Coxswain Duncan Newlands this wild night of pitch blackness, with every light dutifully blacked out in the town, was to locate the wreck. No more exact information than 'the south end of Arran' was available. With the instinct that had already helped him to save many lives the coxswain calculated, from his intimate knowledge of the coast and its tides, that the ship was almost certainly on the Iron Rock Ledges, a fearsome reef that had claimed many a tall ship before.

He estimated the length of time the crossing should take, commensurate with the conditions, at just above an hour. So he pointed the *City*'s bows into the whirling spray, the driving snow and the black lashing dark, and spoke quietly to the engineer. At nine o'clock he ordered the engines to slow ahead, and literally sniffed the air. Former crewmen of Campbeltown's lifeboat are convinced that Duncan Newlands could smell land. However true that may be, on this occasion he ordered a flare sent up; and instantly they all saw, fearful in the red-lit screaming teeth of the gale, the *Dunraven Castle* fast in the dreaded iron grip of the ledges, lying over at a steep angle, pounded by great waves that broke over her, half shrouded in spindrift, sleet and driving snow.

Once more, the coxswain had to rely on his almost magical instinct. The only way to get close and under the lee of the stricken ship was through a narrow rock-strewn passage with a bare two fathoms beneath his keel, and probably lethal rock in the back-wash. In such a position, to think is to act and, once embarked, turning back would have been disastrous.

As so often, the coxswain's instinct was as good as a searchlight and two pairs of eyes. His skill also was superb. Like a racehorse, the boat went through the boiling fearfulness of the narrow passage, taking a few shuddering bumps on the hull, but on smooth rock.

The next task was to approach close enough to the wreck to use the loud hailer to alert the survivors, then to manoeuvre the still wildly tossing boat to such a position that a line could be sent on board, and a wire hawser rigged, down which the trapped men might lower themselves to the heaving lifeboat. Even with a second wire in position, so wild was the heaving that the main wire parted and another had to be rigged by hands now raw and bleeding from contact with the hawser.

Over this line the crew came tumbling to the lifeboat, one by one, half frozen by the snow-laden spindrift, their hands cut by the friction of the cable. The captain came last, just as another wire burst singingly, and the coxswain ordered full speed astern, back out through that narrow gap between the rocks. Once clear and with his course set for Campbeltown Loch far across Kilbrannan Sound, the coxswain ordered a tot of rum for all aboard. He himself had a good pull at the ginger wine, his invariable tipple. The engineer, who was also radio operator, sent out a casual notification of the service completed.

Rather astonishingly, with all that had happened, it was only five minutes after eleven when the *City of Glasgow* put in at the pier, with all twenty-five men from the *Dunraven Castle* safe. There they were met, as always, by the ladies of the Lifeboat Guild, who never fail to be waiting with food, hot drinks and dry clothes. McGrory, the secretary, was always there too— on this occasion in his dual capacity as secretary of the lifeboat and representative of the Shipwrecked Mariners Royal Benevolent Society.

The naval command which had deemed the night too wild for any vessel to go out had been defied; but there is no record of their displeasure.

The 'Byron Darnton' rescue

During March 1946, the *City of Glasgow* was away from Campbeltown undergoing a necessary re-fit. Standing by was a reserve boat *The Duke of Connaught*, a 45ft Watson type, which might best be described as the forerunner of the later Barnett, but with fewer refinements.

The *Duke* was well known to Coxswain Newlands and his crew who had handled her before. She lacked the aid of a searchlight for night-work, she had no radio-telephone, and her engine had frequently proved untrustworthy.

The night of 16 March brought a black gale from the south-east, with patches of darkening sea-fog blanketing the rising waves. Storm cones had been hoisted early. It was the sort of night McGrory's telephone was almost sure to ring. And ring it did, at ten minutes past eleven. The coast-guards at Southend, who work very closely with the lifeboat, reported red flares near Sanda Island three miles or so off the Southend coast.

McGrory ordered the firing of the maroons, which, in Campbeltown, call out not only the lifeboat crew but many townspeople who have had close connection with the sea and its dangers for generations, and can be depended on to be on hand in time of need. It is not idle curiosity that draws them to the edge of the sea, but the natural reaction of people whose fathers, husbands, sons and brothers have always been ruled by the waves.

Coxswain Newlands and his crew got the old *Duke* out and headed round towards Sanda by twenty minutes before midnight. There had been some delay in getting her temperamental engine to respond and now there were clear signs that the gale was increasing in force.

Passing Southend, the coxswain flickered his hand lamp towards the watchful coast-guard, identifying his boat. The coast-guard flickered back in quick code, flashing the information that, to him, it seemed probable that the ship they sought was caught on the Boiler Reef, a notorious line of black rocky fangs running westward into the sea nearly opposite the light-house on the south side of Sanda's isle.

It might appear that things could not have been much worse; while still in comparative shelter, the coxswain now knew he would have to put the old *Duke* into the full path of the gale south of Sanda. But there was even worse to come. Once around

117

the western tip of the isle with the lifeboat fighting both tide-race and gigantic seas, he was able to see, through the flying spindrift, the blazing deck lights of a large vessel. It was close inshore, near the lighthouse, but *inside* the fearsome Boiler Reef.

Coxswain Newlands, knowing every inch of that seaway, even in the dark, stood in as close as possible to the stricken vessel and attempted to draw the attention of anyone who might be on board by sounding the klaxon and flashing his hand lamp. There was neither reply nor sign of life. With her deck lights all ablaze, the doomed vessel lay fast on the reef, pounded by seas that must break her up before long; but as deserted, to all appearances, as the *Marie Celeste*.

The storm was increasing in force by the minute and, after several vain attempts to get any reply to his signals, the coxswain half thought it possible that the lighthouse keepers had somehow already got a line aboard and that the wreck was deserted. In any case, the jagged fangs of rock reaching hungrily from the east end of the reef made it plain that it would be impossible before daylight, in the seas that were running, to get close enough to the strangely silent ship to take off any possible survivors. He decided to make round for a tiny harbour on the north end of the isle, and to attempt to get some information of what had happened from farmers named Russel who lived there.

It was 4 am by the time the lifeboat battered its way round to the anchorage. Snow had come on by now, and in the blackness the farmhouse too seemed deserted. Being without radio it was impossible to communicate with the lighthouse. Coxswain Newlands was uneasy. There might still be someone alive on that stranded ship. With the tide making, just before dawn he put the *Duke* out once more into the teeth of a gale more merciless than ever. One gigantic sea snapped off the rudder bolts and left the boat so helpless that it was with difficulty they were able to stagger back into the lee of the isle to make temporary repairs. Even there, the seas threw the little boat about like a cork. Soon, two of the farm men came down to see what was afoot. They were able to say that, however many were aboard that ship, they were still there. She was the *Byron Darnton*, a 7,000 ton American liberty ship from Copenhagen bound for the United States. She carried a crew of thirty-nine and had fifteen passengers aboard, nine of whom were women.

The coxswain knew that the position demanded urgent action. He sent off five of his crew to run overland to the light-house, where he thought it possible the distressed people might be got off by breeches-buoy equipment. The waiting time must have felt like days. In fact it was only a very short time before the men came racing back, to say that the lighthouse had al-ready offered to rescue those on the *Byron Darnton* by breeches-buoy, but the captain, fearing for the safety of his passengers, was determined to hold on for the lifeboat.

The two farm men, who were also lobster fishers among the the reefs where the ship was caught, valiantly offered to come along and lend their intimate knowledge of the rocks, an offer the coxswain was glad to accept. But now the *Duke*'s engine began playing up again. In the storm, water had been forced by way of the exhaust into the cylinder; with every moment precious, laborious hand cranking had to be resorted to, to get the water out.

At last, it started, if unwillingly; and at last—by now it was nearly noon of the Sunday—with the gale still whipping spray and over mountainous seas, the lifeboat got close enough to the *Byron Darnton* for the coxswain to see that the position was even more desperate than he had earlier feared. The ship was breaking in two, with a large jagged gap already yawning.

All through the night, it transpired later, her radio had been sending out appeals for help; these were picked up and relayed up and down the west coast by everyone except the one lifeboat struggling to the rescue, since the *Duke of Connaught* had no radio-telephone.

Now began the long and hazardous work of getting fifty-four

people off the ship, into the cramped, wildly tossing lifeboat. Coxswain Newlands knew that, if once she broke in two, under the terrible pounding she was taking, there would be little hope of saving many. He also had the awful knowledge at the back of his mind that he was in a desperately dangerous situation, with an engine that might stop at any moment. He could have turned away, for the sure safety of his own men, leaving any chance of rescue to the hope of the storm abating.

He did not do so, of course. He went in, through and among those jagged rocks. The *Byron Darnton*'s boats already hung from the davits, with the women in them, as well as some of the men. This, to Duncan Newlands, looked like a chance. Somehow, with his broken rudder, he worked the *Duke* close underneath the hanging lifeboats, and then yelled to the American captain to lower away. As his order was obeyed and the boats came down, the eager lifeboatmen drew them close and, without too much ceremony, tumbled the distressed passengers into the boat. The women were Norwegian, and a few of the men also. The ship's crew were American.

By now, men were scrambling down the davit falls, some to fall into the heaving water, only to be dragged out again by the strength and skill of the lifeboatmen. One crewman actually had the ship's dog, a small husky, beneath his jacket.

Somehow, in the end, all fifty-four and the dog were accounted for—and not one moment too soon. Even as the coxswain eased the loaded lifeboat out from under the stern of the *Byron Darnton*, the dread sound of rending metal gave clear warning that she was going to break in two at any moment. In the mountainous seas that faced them, lifeboatmen strapped the women securely in. Barely had the boat cleared the turbulent west end of the Boiler Reef when with a rending crash, loud even above the storm, the *Byron Darnton* broke in two, the separate pieces crashing sideways apart into the fury of sea that waited with black fangs bared.

It might have seemed to the coxswain and his men at that

moment, despite their crowded boat and the mountainous seas combined with a strong, racing tide, that the worst of their troubles were over. Then, off the Southend coast, the engine, which had been complaining a lot, cut out altogether. Water had got in again, by way of the exhaust pipes which were mostly submerged due to the heavy load.

Somehow, while the mechanic and the bowman laboured hard over the motor, a lug sail was rigged and under this, with extreme difficulty, the boat clawed on for the next five rolling, tossing miles, often so deep in the trough of the sea that it seemed as if she might never rise again.

Then, in a wild gust, the lug-sail burst to tatters, and anyone but a lifeboatman might have given up then. The almost exhausted rescuers renewed the hard work of trying, while being thrown about, to clear the engine of the water and get it going.

Suddenly, just when they were at their weariest, it coughed into life, and gradually, at half speed, the *Duke* gathered way again. At last, having been at sea for eighteen hours in the worst imaginable conditions, the lifeboat rounded Davaar Island and entered Campbeltown Loch.

As usual, McGrory and the ladies of the Lifeboat Guild, as well as a gathering of townspeople, were waiting to welcome her safe return. They had already made all necessary arrangements for the reception and comfort of the ship's crew and passengers, and an ambulance was standing by to take two of the men to hospital, where beds had been booked for them. There was even food ready for Suzi, the terrified little husky dog—which had, of course, to go into quarantine.

The lifeboatmen went home to their families, after what was to them just another 'service completed'. The men who uphold this tradition of service are not necessarily fishermen or seamen of any kind. They are, purely and simply, lifeboatmen for the hour, and may well be professional and business men in the town, once they peel off their oilskins. In Campbeltown as anywhere, a call for help may not result from the tempests which always mean standing by. Campbeltown lifeboats have conveyed expectant mothers to hospital when roads were impassable. One boat spent a whole night searching Kilbrannan Sound for a dinghy in which two tiring men were being towed out to sea by a giant shark they had succeeded in hooking!

One service is like another. Whatever may be said of young men of today, Campbeltown lifeboat never goes short of volunteers; nor of the pride which all the people of Kintyre have in her.

8   THE ROYAL BURGH

THE visitor to Campbeltown, whether he arrives there by land or by sea, has to have implicit faith in his map; for, almost to the very end of his journey, a round black dot surmounted by the name in block capitals remains the only evidence that there is, in fact, a town of any size within a hundred miles.

The main road from Tarbert leaves the Atlantic coast at Westport, passes through the sleepily ancient village of Kilchenzie with its historic churchyard, and on into the soft green of grazing lands, with here and there a farmyard, and soft-eyed cows tracking the dew-glistening fields. The traveller is just about to conclude that the map-makers have slipped up somehow, and marked in a town where any fool could see no such place exists—when, suddenly, the rolling road tops a slight rise, and there, incredibly close, the spires of the town's many churches rise to eye level out of a wide hollow, open to the loch and the harbour, the substantial nearer buildings cradled by Knock Scalbert's easy slope to the north and bounded southward by the higher, more steeply rising Ben Ghuilean.

The approach from the east side by way of Saddell and Carradale and lovely little Peninver discovers the town with perhaps even more dramatic suddenness. All the winding narrow way, the senses have been drugged by the sheer beauty of the broken coastline, the blue width of Kilbrannan Sound reaching across to Arran's mountains, then opening to the bluer hazier width of the firth, where the coast of Ayrshire dreams in the sunlight. Climbing the long slow hill by Kilchousland's grey mouldering stones, Davaar Island looms startlingly close, like a great brown whale asleep on a sea where only the call of the wheeling gulls ever breaks the silence. Then, suddenly once again, the top of Trench Point—and there lies the Royal Burgh of Campbeltown, all a-throng with industry and commerce, shrouded by a rare passing shower, or brooding beneath the softly dispersing smoke-haze that rings the higher towers.

Perhaps it is to the traveller who arrives by sea that the old grey town presents its most welcoming face. Sailing northward from the Mull, Davaar Island with its lighthouse has to be rounded before Campbeltown comes into view, still far enough away to soften the hard lines of the more recent housing developments. Arriving by way of Kilbrannan Sound, and rounding Trench Point, the eye is caught by the colourful bustle of fishing craft and small boats in the bay or around the quay, so that, for a time, Campbeltown is but a background which, after a second or a third glance, may be regarded as the best possible kind of town to be just where it is.

For the leisurely holidaymaker, the 134 mile road from Glasgow to Campbeltown can be claimed to pass through some of the finest scenery in the West Highlands; it can also take a minimum of $4\frac{1}{2}$ hours to cover, even non-stop. Flying time from Glasgow is only a quarter of an hour, plus a ten-minute run from the airport.

THE WEE TOON

Heart and centre of Campbeltown, even if not geographically, is the famed Campbeltown Cross, recognised as the finest specimen of late medieval carving in the rich field of Kintyre.

The carved monument of blue chlorite-schist, regarded by experts as a stone likely to have its origin in the Loch Sween area of Mid Argyll, has occupied its splendid position near the head of the Old Quay since the end of World War II. Before that time, and very likely since the early seventeenth century, it stood as Campbeltown's Market Cross high up the Main Street, outside the town hall.

Page 125 Business and Pleasure: (*above*) the puffer *Warlight*, one of a dwindling fleet on which the economy of the isles used to depend, loading timber at Tarbert; (*below*) the *Duchess of Hamilton*, well loaded with summer day-trippers at Campbeltown

Page 126 (*above*) The trade of sailmaking has been carried on for centuries in Kintyre. Here, Andrew Lietch of Tarbert cuts by hand a sail which may be on order for a customer in the Fijis, or San Francisco, or even Carradale; (*below*) women at work in Tarbert's modern sea-food factory. Here the scallop shells are opened, the tiny edible portions of the shell-fish cut out, packed and frozen. This delicacy is almost exclusively for export, mostly to the USA

It is a typical but specially fine example of the Iona school of stone carving, now thought to date from the fourteenth century and not the fifteenth, as was for long believed. The inscription, in Latin relief, is what gives the clue to its age. Translated, it reads: 'This is the cross of Sir Ivor MacEachern, sometime parson of Kilkivan, and of his son, Sir Andrew, parson of Kilchoman, who caused it to be made'. Now, Kilchoman is in Islay, but a parson named Andrew MacEachern was translated to that parish from Kilkivan near Campbeltown about 1375. It is highly probable that this was the Andrew Mac-Eachern who had the cross set up, not at Campbeltown—which did not come into existence as Lochhead till about two and a half centuries later—but at Kilkivan, whence it was later removed to the newly founded lowland burgh to serve as the market cross there.

From its ancient stance in Main Street, it was taken down for safety during World War II, when the presence of shipping in the wide harbour gave rise to attack by German bombers. The new, permanent site for the cross enhances its dignity and allows of more leisurely appreciation of the singular beauty of the complicated, twining foliage, the grace in stone of the carved human and animal figures. While the bulk of the carving is in surprisingly excellent condition, there are clear signs of deliberate erasure, especially in the case of what was obviously a representation of the crucifixion. This type of vandalism was considered praiseworthy at the time of the Reformation, when many beautifully carved crucifixion scenes in stone were broken up by religiously zealous Presbyterians.

By long tradition, all funerals, from whatever part of the town, are routed to pass by the cross; and each midnight on Hogmanay—31 December—the New Year is welcomed in under its ancient shadow.

From the cross, Main Street runs straight up to Castlehill. This broad, well-planned street contains three of the town's four hotels and many of the principal shops. Main Street's

H

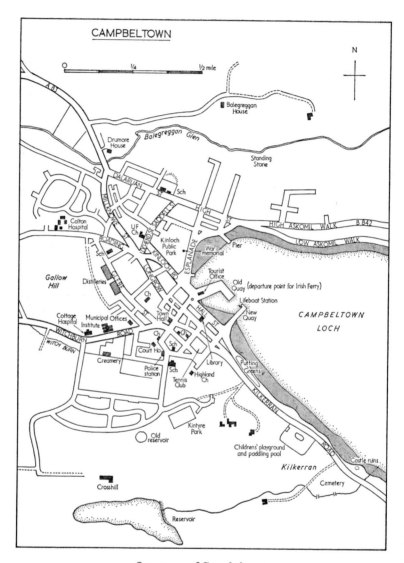

Street map of Campbeltown

gradient is gently deceptive. At its head on Castlehill stand the police station, sheriff court and Castlehill church sharing the eminent site of the one-time Earl of Argyll's splendid castle—and possibly sharing some of its totally untraceable stones also.

The church of Castlehill, founded in 1778, replaced the earlier Lowland church which, nowadays a church hall in Kirk Street, was built in 1706 to replace the first Lowland kirk—known as the Thatched House—founded on the same site in 1654. Kirk Street runs off to the left from Main Street, and the church hall stands where lies buried that Elizabeth Tollemache, first Duchess of Argyll, who gave her black and silver love knot to the Campbeltown coat of arms. The present-day imposing Castlehill church was, incidentally, built by an Inveraray architect, and the master stonemason came from that town also. It cost £1,258 14s 10d—probably rather less than its present minister might expect to pay for a car.

A little way down Main Street from Castlehill stands the comparatively modern town hall. It was completed in 1760 on the site of the earlier Tolbooth outside which the market cross used to stand, and before which citizens of the burgh were called to assemble whenever a proclamation of any sort was to be read out. The present graceful spire of the building replaced the original timber-built one in 1778. In the museum in Hall Street hangs a painting, by Alexander MacKinnon of the Davaar Cave painting fame, which vividly recalls the somewhat riotous market day scenes in Main Street, close by the town hall, around the mid-nineteenth century.

From this point Kirk Street, which now runs by way of a tennis club towards Stronvaar bowling green, long ago ended at the door of the original Gaelic church, founded there in 1642. The present Gaelic church of Campbeltown replaced this earlier building only in 1806. It stands square and solid today, though its steeple has collapsed twice—in 1830 and 1884—due mostly to the church heritors' original insistence on its design being changed after its construction was half way to being completed!

Most of the other streets of Campbeltown proper spread their arms out from Main Street which was the first part of the burgh to be laid out. Chief and busiest of these is Longrow South, a thronging shopping centre which, almost within living memory, was a narrow, insanitary alley of tall tenements leaning towards each other; old pictures show strings of washing stretching across from house to house. It was known then as 'the Wide Close', and until comparatively recent times elderly people referred to Longrow South as New Street.

It is a wide, pleasant street of excellent shops nowadays, joining Longrow proper at Reform Square and becoming the main road to the west coast and on to Tarbert. Reform Square, incidentally, takes its name purely from use and wont, and not by any council decision, from the fact that in 1832 some of the most fervent supporters of the First Reform Bill had their homes there.

On every hand in Campbeltown, street and place names recall the past. Just where Longrow becomes the north-west road, there is Millknowe, the site of a mill dam but now a housing scheme. On the right hand nearby, Parliament Place marks the site of a one-time parliament firmly convened by a Scottish king. Gallow Hill speaks grimly for itself; Dalaruan Street marks a very early Scots settlement. The Big Kiln tells its own story, as does the Witch Burn—even if nobody knows who were the witches who gave it its name or whether the burn was just a useful place for ducking them.

Kilkerran Road, with its waving palms, running along the shore from the New Quay towards Davaar, certainly perpetuates the name of Ciaran, that gentle friend and early mentor of Columba—whose cave, containing a stone water bowl and altar, is traditionally believed to be the largest of a group on this coast road, about $3\frac{1}{2}$ miles beyond the ruins of the castle built near the shore by James IV in 1498. On the opposite side of the road lies the extremely ancient but still used cemetery in the heart of which stood the saint's earliest church, its remains, though the site is known, no longer traceable on the ground

Dalintober—place of the well—was not all that long ago a village on its own, disconnected entirely from the burgh, not only administratively, but physically by a deep muddy sand inlet of the loch known as the Mussel Ebb, which was only reclaimed by a massive filling-in operation in 1876. The pleasant open space thus provided was laid out as Kinloch Park with playing fields and public tennis courts. Facing the broad Esplanade which runs towards Dalintober stands the name-crammed war memorial. At the end of the Esplanade, High Askomil Walk carries the road to Carradale on the east side steeply out over the burgh boundary; while, from Dalintober, Low Askomil skirts the shore to the ship yard of Trench Point, and beyond to the Maiden's Planting and Macringan's Point.

AMENITIES AND SERVICES

Statistically, Campbeltown differs little from any semi-industrial, residential, educational fishing port and shopping centre to be found anywhere in the mainland of Scotland—except that there is no other town quite like it anywhere.

It is a royal burgh, of course; from its early seventeenth-century foundations, it now embraces an area of 1,517·8 acres, the town council having built almost a thousand new homes from the close of World War II up to 1971. At the last count, the population stood at 6,045.

As befits a town that for long drew its wealth from the sea, places of worship are plentiful, ranging from four large churches of Scotland, by way of St Kieran's Roman Catholic and Episcopal churches, to both United Free and Free Church of Scotland, as well as the Brethren with their hall in Well Close, and the Salvation Army which has its brightly painted citadel tucked away in Burnside Street.

The one police station commands the main part of the town from the eminence of Castlehill, not far from the post office, the town hall and the courthouse. The town's single newspaper, the *Campbeltown Courier*, established in 1871, has its office in the Longrow. Near the head of the pier stands a well-appointed information office, manned all the year round. In Hall Street, leading to Kilkerran Road, the putting greens and the children's paddling pool, a somewhat unpretentious red sandstone building houses Campbeltown's library and museum. The museum contains exhibits ranging from the very earliest flint arrowheads and stone axes up to fascinatingly detailed models of famous steamers and Campbeltown lifeboats of the past. Nearby are the town's two spacious cinemas.

Always famed for its educational facilities, Campbeltown now has the county's most modern grammar school, situated in the vicinity of the Lime Craigs, and not far from Kintyre Park. Besides the town itself, the catchment area of this school extends over a very large part of the peninsula.

Local government is vested in the town council, which is made up of a provost, two baillies, a dean of guild, treasurer and twelve councillors. Health services are of a high standard, the four local hospitals being under their own board of management, with a ready and swift air ambulance service on call at all times for urgent cases demanding transfer to larger city hospitals.

HOLIDAY ATTRACTIONS

A seaside town flanked and almost surrounded by beaches of gold and silver, with many square miles of freely accessible open hills, with lochs and rivers well stocked, and the most compact array of historical and prehistoric monuments to be found anywhere in the land—how could such a town, which boasts a daily average of four hours' sunshine, fail to hold something for every imaginable kind of holiday resident?

Sport and recreation

What if one wished to spend every day playing golf? Few such people have not heard of the world-famous links of Machrihanish and Dunaverty, and there is also the most attractive little nine-hole course at Carradale. For tennis enthusiasts, there is the fine court of the Campbeltown Lawn Tennis Club in St John Street, as well as the public tennis courts in Kinloch Park. Football is played at two parks, Kinloch and Kintyre. Perhaps to reassure such visitors as may have read of Kintyre's turbulent past, the game of cricket has been established in recent years and, as in other outposts, appears to have taken firm root. There are two excellent, friendly bowling greens, and two putting greens in Kilkerran Road. Not far away are the children's spacious paddling pool, swings and chutes; while safe, most attractive bathing and paddling beaches for children are within reach at Dalintober and Kilkerran.

The active local sailing club makes visitors welcome and many participate in regularly arranged racing. Frequent motor-boat trips operate within the loch where small rowing boats are also available for hire. A branch of the Scottish Surf Club is based on Machrihanish, where towering crested rollers provide rare facilities for this sport.

The angler is particularly well catered for. Where small rivers sing through remote yet easily accessible glens, salmon, sea trout and brown trout give lively sport in beautiful surroundings. Fees for permit are low; indeed, Machrihanish Water, far from being least among the salmon and sea-trout rivers of Kintyre, may be fished without any charge whatsoever.

Nearby lochs are kept well stocked with trout. On four of these, Crosshill, Lussa, Auchalochy and Tangy, boats are available for hire; Lochruan is fished from the bank. Here again permit fees are low; information as to where permits may be obtained is readily available either from the angling club or at the information centre on the pier—where details of excellent sea-angling facilities may also be had.

Entertainment

Naturally there are those visitors who would regard participation in such recreations as needless expenditure of energy. For them, the town's entertainments committee lays on, every summer, an increasing range of spectator items, from Highland Games by way of regattas and film shows to dancing, concerts and Gaelic ceilidh. The ceilidh, in its origin, was the meeting of a few neighbours in one house or the other, for story, song, fiddle-playing and courting—the latter activity being more pleasantly pursued in a dimly-lit corner of a peat-hazed room than on the shelterless moor or the open windswept shore. The ceilidh, in both the concert and modern versions, is provided by the town's Gaelic choir, many times winner of the highest award at the National Mod—the Gaelic musical festival. Visitors so minded are given the opportunity to take part in the ceilidh, according to ancient tradition. The frequent appearance of the kilted pipe-band must also rank high as a spectacle and a sound to stir the heart of any tourist.

Expeditions

For many Campbeltown will prove to be a charming centre for local exploration—as far north as, say, Tayinloan and including the Isle of Gigha. The explorer does not need a car. Bus services are good, and many of the points most worthy of a visit are seen to best advantage by the traveller on foot. A climb to the top of Ben Ghuilean is for the more energetic, but the reward in the form of width of prospect is generous. By the way, this hill must, in Campbeltown, be pronounced as if spelt 'Bengullion'! Most local people actually spell it that way. More leisurely are the gentler hill walks in the vicinity, by quiet lochs and ancient standing stones; by the shingled shell-crusted Dorlinn, at low tide, to Davaar's Isle, or, at the other end of the bay, beyond Dalintober, by Trench Point to the famed Black Rocks.

By car, perhaps the loveliest road of all is that leaving the town by way of Kilkerran, continuing on beyond the Dorlinn and the crumbling bones of James IV's fine castle to the extraordinarily named Glen of New Orleans, by small, singing, tumbling streams where wild flowers spill in cascades almost on to the road.

By Auchenhoan Head of St Ciaran's cave, the narrowing old road winds above the Sound, steep and twisting in places, but providing at every turn a prospect of blue sea, golden shore and lazily breaking waves, each more breath-catchingly beautiful than the last. This is not the main road to Southend—which leaves town by way of Lorne Street and is modern, wide and straight—but the one-time drove track to the same destination, 'the learside', probably the leeward side, as it is known locally.

The Isle of Sanda, early foothold of the Danish rovers, with its tiny attendant Sheep Isle, lies like a green gem on the sea's breast out from the golden beaches divided by MacShannon's Point, before the narrow track dips to Southend and bloodstoried Dunaverty, its mighty rock cut off from the headland as by the stroke of some gigantic axe.

Not far from here, an open-air service is held every year early in summer at Keil, where stand the crumbling ruins of one of Kintyre's many ancient chapels, and where it is not improbable that Columba landed on a visit to his old friend, Ciaran, and his relatives on the throne of Dalriada.

From Keil to the lighthouse at the Mull, the ever narrowing road winds upward through what is surely the most desolate, yet the grandest scenery in all Kintyre. Here, where on a still day the song of the lark is loud in the silence and eagles wheel majestically against the blue, the telegraph poles leading to the Mull have to be kept only hand-high in order to stand firm against the fierce storm-winds that, in winter, scream over these now hushed hills.

Machrihanish of the golf is reached more easily. Here there is the widest expanse of firm golden beach in Kintyre. Here, too, for the walker is the incomparably breathtaking view of the rock-bound Cauldrons—'Gauldrons' in the local idiom— where, even on a still day, mighty rollers break with a deafening crash and, on a day of storm, send white spindrift flying far inland over the cliffs. Westward, through the haze that in summer softens the blue of the sea, the isles of Islay and Gigha lie startlingly close, with the mountains of Jura piercing the skies farther north.

On the east side, Carradale of the woods and glens, the green ways and the fishing boats, is also within easy reach. Here was the last outpost of spoken Gaelic in Kintyre; and here, incidentally, is based yet another choir which has always given a good account of itself at the National Mod.

HOME TOWN

Pleasant as Campbeltown can be as a holiday centre, it must surely have something for the six to seven thousand people who choose to spend their lives there. First and foremost, there is the fierce pride of belonging, though not often consciously, to a town cut off, geographically, from other centres of population, that has survived one industrial depression after another, and despite all the odds stacked against it has come up smiling, quick to rejoice in the sunshine of prosperity, yet with a cautious Highland eye open for sign of any new cloud on the horizon. These are a people who built their own town, who raked the seven seas in days gone by for commerce to keep its chimneys smoking; who knew success and failure, and were prepared to make the best of both in turn; who can close their ranks with firm purpose, and still hold out a welcoming hand to the stranger.

Such is Kintyre's royal burgh. *Ignavis precibus fortuna repugnat* runs its motto, which may be roughly translated as 'Fortune helps who help themselves'—a truth which has been clear to the burghers of Campbeltown from the day they first set about gathering stones to build their town. It has a long, turbulent history at its back. Home of a mixed race whose forebears, tested in the fire of many wars, have been welded firmly into one people, neither Highland nor Lowland; a people—and this is true for all of Kintyre—who can look back with pride in past achievement, and forward with that brand of confidence in their own worth which has overcome so many difficulties already.

9 DISCOVERING KINTYRE

THE visitor to Kintyre should, if it were possible, employ no fewer than three pairs of eyes in looking for what this 'best of the isles' has to show. The archaeological treasure-house contained within its borders is sufficient to test one pair; another is needed to watch its stormy and never predictable history unfolding. The third and perhaps most important pair would be kept zealously undimmed for the enjoyment of a wider variety of land and seascapes than may be found anywhere else in Scotland.

Kintyre holds tree-shadowed ways where filtered sunlight dapples the flower-starred green, and the scuffle of a blackbird in the dry leaves sounds loud in the cathedral hush of noon. It holds, even on the same day, heather-bending tempests over frowning sea-wet crags, where the scream of the wind is broken only by the thunderous, land-shaking roar of green seas breaking white on hungry black fangs of rock that gleam angrily in the hissing back-wash before the next mighty roller comes crashing from the world's end. And it holds everything between.

TARBERT

The natural stepping-off place for a tour of Kintyre is Tarbert, where the signboard bidding the visitor welcome is as often as not almost completely hidden by the riot of golden broom that spills from the road verge down towards the attractively land-locked little harbour. From this height the small town comes into view too suddenly for the eye to take in everything at once.

138

The instant impression is of colour: the gold of the broom, the purple of the ling and heather clothing the slopes, and the well-painted shop fronts curving away to the left around the sickle of bay, beneath pleasant houses that seem to cling to the crags above. In the foreground white-winged gulls lean idly on the soft wind that sends vari-coloured sails skimming across the blue inner harbour, against the wall of which lie the fishing boats. Above all else broods the ivy-mantled ruin of an ancient strong tower.

Paps of Jura

This is the building known as 'Bruce's Castle', for want of a better name; it stood on its high rock before the twelfth century, but it is true that Scotland's hero king repaired it and added much to its structure. From its broken walls, reached by a winding but not too difficult path above the police station, can be seen the best view of Tarbert and its harbour.

The neat row of fishermen's cottages along the front speaks of the little town's early dependence on the sea; while the small houses and bungalows clinging, along with scrub birch, to ledges in the rocky slopes above point to its desirability as just a place to live. Rising out of the smoke haze that always seems to hang over the harbour, the tall gothic-crowned tower of the church looks towards both seas, standing as it does beside the highest point of the road across the isthmus.

Like so many once thriving fishing ports, Tarbert leans heavily on the tourist industry nowadays. It has three first-class hotels, many boarding houses and bed and breakfast places. Golf, tennis, bowls and sea-fishing are all laid on, and for the less energetically inclined visitor it is a pleasant place in which to stroll, especially along the South Quay. There, on conveniently placed seats, it is easy and restful to get into conversation with fishermen of an earlier day, watching their sons and grandsons preparing to put to sea in less numerous but better equipped boats.

The road southward into Kintyre proper follows not the ancient shipping drag track but the hill on the Kilberry side, giving yet another restful view of the quiet land-locked harbour, before almost immediately dropping to sea level again at the West Loch. It is a good broad road, bypassing MacBrayne's ancient Islay terminal and skirting the coast past Kennacraig of Western Ferries, with small caravan sites discreetly tucked under trees here and there. This is the west-side road that carries all the commercial traffic to Campbeltown. By crossing to the east side at the first opportunity, the visitor will be following the sun all day, finding it topping the peaks of Arran in the morning, warming the rocks of the rugged Mull at noon and still high over Islay and Jura on the return journey northward in the evening.

The opportunity to cross over comes just south of the ferry terminal at Kennacraig, where a clearly signposted single-track road goes off sharply to the left to climb over the moorland spine of the peninsula to Kilbrannan Sound. Passing places are frequent and always being improved upon, but a caravan trailer of any size can prove an embarrassment on such a road as this.

The highest point of it demands a stop, where first the marching, jagged peaks of Arran come into view, almost startlingly close. Against the morning sky these mountains give the impression of being cut out of hard blue steel rather than formed from rock; while westward, out of the Atlantic haze, Islay and rugged Jura seem much softer of outline and farther away than they really are. Below, where the narrow ribbon of road winds down and down, white-capped wavelets intensify the blue of the sea where Kilbrannan Sound washes the softly golden sands of Claonaig.

SKIPNESS

The south-bound road does not descend to the sands that cradle the ferry terminal for Arran. But it is well worth while to go right down there, so close to the beach that the soft sand drifts over the narrow road, turning northward again through great weather-worn natural monoliths of rock to Skipness, a village where a stream, loud in the silence, tumbles from its wooded glen to empty along the curving shore. No visitor can resist the enchantment of this remote spot; nor fail to wonder why no signpost tells of its existence.

Skipness—from the Norse, 'Ship Point'—has not been of even the slightest economic importance for about nine hundred years, when it was the ideal landing place for such Norse rovers as wished to make a foray into either Kintyre or Knapdale. Those plunderers probably set up a shore base, which was settled as a peaceful village when Somerled broke the Norse hold on Kintyre. In its almost noonday hush, Skipness gives the distinct impression of not having changed all that much since then.

Beyond the tree-shaded stone bridge spanning the burn, an avenue of ancient hardwoods leads to the crumbling but immensely durable ruins of Skipness Castle. This dignified building has an air of splendour that even the nettles which grow everywhere about it cannot take away. As far back as

1246, it was the residence of one Dugfallas, son of Syfyn, who in that year presented his adjacent chapel of St Columba by charter to Paisley Abbey. In 1261, extensions to the castle's curtain wall encroached on the chapel causing its partial demolition. To compensate for this, another chapel—dedicated to St Brendan who gave his name to the Sound between here and Arran—was built to seaward, overlooking a quiet bay with fine views of both Arran and Bute. This old chapel, easily accessible by walking around the shore, is well worth a visit, being in a good state of preservation and of architectural interest.

The castle itself, of square Norman style forming a rectangle of roughly 40 by 28yd, has three projecting towers and a keep. It owes its long existence and present state of preservation to its enormously thick walls and the strange circumstances that it was never subjected to any prolonged siege. It is built from local stone—micaschist; while the dressed quoins at the angles and door and window lintels are formed of red sandstone which was clearly brought across from Arran. The earliest part of this old stronghouse is probably the north-west corner, which may have been part of the original simpler house of 1220 or so, when Donald, grandson of Somerled, was Lord of Islay and virtual King of Kintyre.

Leaving the castle gates, the narrow road winds two miles farther north-eastward from the bridge, over a stretch of moorland alive with bird-life and wild flowers, to the sea again, where the ruins of a one-time steamer pier look across to Bute. In days long past, this pier formed a link between Skipness and the outside world, but the change to road transport caused the structure to be abandoned to the storms which have reduced it to its stone-built foundations.

Leaving the village again, to climb the little way upward to the east-side road into Kintyre, the visitor may wonder about the economy of this backwater, where there has been no crofting as such for over a hundred years and the fishing industry was

Page 143   (*above*) Interior of a farm cottage at the turn of the century. Note the box beds let into the wall, and the treasured toys; (*below*) a kitchen interior of the same period. These interiors are preserved in the Museum of Farming Life at Auchendrain in Mid Argyll

Page 144 (*above*) 'Dolls' house' dwellings at Killean. These tiny non-traditional houses were built to the fancy of an estate owner, and attract much attention from tourists; (*below*) in complete contrast, the homes built for RAF servicemen at Machrihanish

wound up at the beginning of the present century. The answer, for the depleted population, is found in back-lying farms, mostly out of sight from the road, some forestry work and, perhaps most of all, the tourist industry.

EAST KINTYRE

Southward from Skipness, the narrow road climbs steeply, only to plunge crazily downward again, upward and downward, with ever more breathtaking views of Arran around every twisted humpbacked old stone bridge. It is a road that was clearly engineered for the horse-drawn vehicle, to serve the hill farms on either hand, where from patchwork fields soft-eyed cattle thoughtfully contemplate the passers-by. Here and there, where the road winds downward close to the sea are lovely bays of silver sands and lazily breaking waves.

Crossaig, Cour and Grogport—there is little to choose for restful beauty between these three bays, with the view across to Arran becoming clearer with every mile. At Grogport, a most attractive village right on the beach, rustic bench seats and tables have been placed at several suitable pull-in points, to add to the enjoyment of an outdoor meal.

The road-builders must surely have been unwilling to leave this supremely pleasant village. When the road does take its departure, it winds back in corkscrew fashion, and back again in a series of hairpin bends, climbing for 300ft into Carradale Forest, whence it swoops downward once more into the long lovely wooded glen of Carradale Water.

The river here is Kintyre's biggest stream and among the county's finest salmon fishings. The road, as it descends the glen, passes through sun-dappled avenues of varied hardwoods in every conceivable shade of green, with the entire hillside far away to the right a blaze of red and pink from massed rhododendrons.

The road widens just a little at this point making it easier to find the village of Carradale, which lies, well signposted, off the main road to the south. Its neat new style houses cluster around and above the harbour which, with its modern pier completed in 1959, is the base for the fourteen or so fishing boats operating mainly in the Sound. Fishing is still an important part of Carradale's economy, though around twenty fairly big farms carry both sheep and cattle, with dairy herds dependent on the creamery at Campbeltown. The tourist industry is also very much on the increase.

Carradale harbour

Here are several of the finest sandy beaches in Kintyre, perhaps the best being Carradale Bay itself, accessible through the grounds of Carradale House, whose beautiful gardens are open to the public daily from April to September. At the outer end of this bay, on a rocky tidal islet that detaches itself from a stubby peninsula, can be seen the remains of a most excellent example of a circular vitrified fort. Up till now only about fifty such vitrified forts have been discovered in the whole country, and two of them are in Kintyre; the second being less easily

visited in its lofty position over on the west side, above the
village of Clachan. Caesar's *Gallic Wars* carries descriptions of
similar fortifications in France, where timber, possibly peat and
other combustibles were presumably built into the heart of
the stone walls, then deliberately set alight with the object of
fusing or vitrifying the entire structure, giving to it a strength
which no projectile known in the first century, when they were
built, was likely to breach.

THE MOUNTAIN OF THE BOAR

Overlooking Carradale Bay from the west, Beinn an Tuirc
(Mountain of the Boar) rises to 1,491ft, the highest point in
Kintyre. Its name commemorates the last sad exploit of the
Fingalian hero, Diarmid, who is said to have been the progenitor
of the Campbell clan. The Fingalians were a legendary race of
heroes who inhabited Argyll about the dawn of history. Their
leader was Fionn Mac Cumhal, often referred to as Fingal.

The story is told of how Grainne, beautiful daughter of King
Cormac, was preparing for her wedding to Fionn himself, when
she fell hopelessly in love with the young hero, Diarmid. She
begged him to run away with her, but this Diarmid flatly
refused to do, out of loyalty to his chief and for the love that
was strong between him and Fionn. Instead he went off alone,
wandering in the fastnesses of Kintyre. Grainne, now Fionn's
wife, crazed by her love, followed Diarmid and found him
there.

The Fingalians, meantime, believed Diarmid dead; till on a
day of hunting, they found sign of him in the woods. Fionn
himself raised the hunting cry, knowing that, if he were indeed
alive, Diarmid could not but reply. Grainne, hearing the call
ring through the woods, begged Diarmid not to make answer;
but he, safe in his mind that he had treated the lovely Grainne
always as a sister, sent his own call ringing back, and presently
he was in the midst of the rejoicing Fingalians. Over the camp

fire that night, Fionn told Diarmid of a great boar they had that day followed, and challenged him to face it in the hunt.

The chase was long, next day, but finally, though the great beast fought furiously and bent Diarmid's tempered blade like a rush, the young hero overcame it and it lay dead. Fionn furrowed his brow. It had been his hope that this boy whom he had loved might meet a hunter's honourable death in the chase.

'Measure the boar,' he commanded. And, joyfully, Diarmid paced the beast from snout to tail.

'Sixteen feet!' he called triumphantly.

Fionn shook his head. 'Not so,' he doubted. 'Measure him again—the other way!'

So Diarmid paced again, this time against the lie of the poisonous bristles, one of which pierced the vulnerable mole on his bare foot, so that he fell mortally wounded.

Fionn, seized by remorse at the young hero's agony, cried out, 'What can I do, Diarmid, to heal your wound?'

'A draught from yonder spring,' Diarmid begged, 'carried in your own hands.'

Fionn raced to the spring, and filled his cupped hands. But even as he rose, his thoughts flickered momentarily on the beauty of Grainne and he let the water spill through his fingers.

Diarmid called weakly, and Fionn filled his cupped hands again. But again the thought of his lost love made his hands shake with anger, so that the water spilled away.

Yet a third time, Fionn filled his hands with the healing water, and this time, pushing all else from his mind, rushed to Diarmid's side, begging the young man to drink quickly. But Diarmid lay dead; and deep was the grief of Fionn at this slaying of the flower of all his band. Deeper still was his rage when the Fingalians appeared with Grainne, whom they had found in the woods, and he learnt that, in all their wanderings, Diarmid had treated her with the honour due to the wife of his chief. He refused even to look on her, but ordered that she be put to death instantly, for her faithlessness and deceit.

On the crest of the Campbell clan there is a boar's head which—it may be—was earned for them on that day.

SADDELL ABBEY

Back on the main road, the village of Saddell lies in its own deep glen, so tucked away in the woods one might pass it by and never notice. Yet this sleepy little place was once of very great ecclesiastic importance in Argyll. The one-time Cistercian abbey, hidden up to the right beside a singing burn, may well have been founded by Somerled himself in 1160, and one of the tombs within the ruins is believed to be his resting place. Certainly he had a close connection with Saddell, for in a Paisley charter, his son Reginald is named as the abbey's founder. According to story handed down by bards over the centuries, Reginald journeyed to Rome where he gathered a quantity of consecrated dust which he scattered on the soil where the foundations of the abbey were laid.

The singing burn, beside which only fragments of the once stately building now stand, is still called Allt nam Monach, the Monks' Burn. It flows quietly today—just as it must always have done—down through Bealach nam Marbh (the Pass of the Dead) over which were borne the bodies of the faithful from the west side for burial here. The extent of the dignified ground plan is now difficult to trace, though it is clear that the original building was of graceful proportions. What is also clear is that its present fragmented condition is largely due to the spoilation to which its walls were subjected in the building of nearby Saddell House—a process of vandalistic quarrying sadly not uncommon in the West Highlands even up to the nineteenth century.

In what was once the choir lie a number of beautifully carved and sculptured tombstones and slabs, with elaborate ornamentation in the shape of figures from life, hounds, stags, swords, galleys and shears. The effigies of armed warriors are among the finest to be found, even in Argyll.

149

Over the ancient site rests an indefinable air of quiet peace, which makes the visitor wish to linger.

KILCHOUSLAND

Southward from Saddell the hills fall away into wider fields as woodland diminishes and agricultural land opens richly broad in its acres. Just two miles out from Campbeltown, but not yet in sight of even a church spire of that town, the ancient ruined church of Kilchousland, with its surrounding burial ground, comes into view on the left almost on the edge of a steep cliff above the shore.

This ancient roofless building well merits a visit, if only for the extreme beauty of its setting. The great hills of Arran are now to the left, as one faces the church, with beyond them to the south the blue outline of the Ayrshire coast and Ailsa Craig rising out of the mists of the Firth of Clyde; and, right in the blue foreground, the dark brown hump of Davaar Island guarding the entry to Campbeltown Loch.

The church, of which most of the side walls and about all the west gable still stand, measured about 60ft by 20ft. It is surrounded by many very interesting carved stones of varying antiquity—with a notable lack, however, of the 'many fragments of elegant crosses' which the *Third Statistical Account*, of 1791, speaks of as being so numerous as to have given the adjacent farm its name of Crossiby. Also completely vanished is a notable stone described in that same account and seen in the churchyard by Peter MacIntosh, whose *History of Kintyre* was published about a hundred years later.

This stone, much sought after in recent times because of its romantic associations, is described as a rude pillar with a hole in its centre big enough for a hand to pass through. Eloping lovers who were able to reach the old church and join hands through the hole were regarded as lawfully married. The custom prevailed, in the words of the *Statistical Account*, 'till

150

almost the present day'—1791. This simple method of binding appears to have been approved of by St Couslan himself, since his ruling was that a promise of marriage was as absolutely indissoluble as any legal ceremony could ever be.

Stone rubbing of a galley, one of the many fine drawings to be found in Kintyre churchyards

His stringent views were not shared by his neighbour St Coivan, whose church of Kilkivan stands in a similar ruinous state about $4\frac{1}{2}$ miles beyond Campbeltown towards Machrihanish. This jolly ecclesiastic—who incidentally lived to the age of 120 years—held that those wedded couples who did not find themselves in complete agreement should meet at his church at midnight on a stated day each year, when he would conduct

a reshuffle. His way of carrying this out was to blindfold everyone there and, on the stroke of midnight, to chase them round
the outside of the church three times, before shouting the word
Gabhag—that is, 'seize' or 'take to you'. At this, every man,
blindfold, had to grab hold of whatever female he could get a
hand on; and there and then each was fitted out with a wife
who, good or bad, plain or fancy, was his till the annual reshuffle
came round again—when, of course, he might have no wish to
attend.

CAMPBELTOWN AND DAVAAR ISLAND

The road climbs fairly steeply away from Kilchousland, topping
the rise of Trench Point, from where the Royal Burgh of
Campbeltown (see Chapter 8) can be better viewed than from
anywhere on land or sea. From this hill the strong curving
width of Campbeltown Loch can be seen driving a full $2\frac{1}{2}$ miles
into the inner haven, sheltered by the great green and brown
hump of Davaar Island, with the dark scythe of strand uncovered at low tide between it and the mainland at Kilkerran.
At the very heart and forefront of the town is the busy harbour,
square with its two quays, and the commercial section of the
burgh crowding above and about it, rising, speared by church
towers and spires, to Castlehill with the land beyond that still
lifting greenly to the bulk of Ben Ghuilean at 1,154ft.

This first view of Campbeltown is affected, naturally, by
weather. On a grey rainy day, it can seem a not-too-well
planned huddle of buildings around and above a wide bay
that might have been made a place of beauty. Against a blue
sky, on the other hand, the beauty is all there—in the grey age
of the place, in the haze of smoke that lingers among the pointed
spires, and in the curving width of the finest anchorage in all
the west.

The road leading in from Trench Point skirts the playing
fields, passes the ancient town cross and makes its broad palm-
fringed way round the curve of the bay towards Kilkerran.

About two miles along the Kilkerran road, the long, curving shingle causeway, known as An Dorlinn, sweeps out for three-quarters of a mile, at low tide, to the island of Davaar. This isle, deserted save for its lighthouse on the northern tip, is famed for the large cave painting of the crucifixion which mysteriously appeared there in 1887. It was later found to have been the secret work of a local artist Alexander MacKinnon, who returned to Kintyre in the early 1930s, when he was eighty years old, to re-touch it.

The cave of the painting is fifth in a line of seven which cleave the great cliffs of the isle. Near to its entrance filtered sunlight touching the many coloured wild rock plants brings a sense of restful serenity to the cool vaulted cavern, which echoes to the lowest whisper. The colours of the larger-than-life painting on the rock wall are, though fading with time, still in harmony with the cathedral-like surroundings, and one inevitably wonders what it was that prompted a young man, long ago, to come over here secretly and alone to create this work.

Even if the long shingle causeway to the isle appears safely dry, it must be stressed that the difficult, almost mile-long walk from Kilkerran takes time and when the tide turns it races fast. The fortunate visitor is one who finds himself safely marooned on Davaar to await the next ebb. The temptation to attempt the return trip with perhaps a knee-deep soaking is one to be avoided at all costs. It is all too easy to lose the curving crest of the shingle, in which event there is no turning back or pressing on, but only the hope of one more rescue to add to a long list. Advice about tide times can be obtained from the information bureau on the pier at Campbeltown.

SOUTHEND AND THE MULL

To visit the village of Southend and from there the ultimate tip of the Mull of Kintyre, the time-saving way is to return to

Campbeltown and take the short ten-mile inland route. A feast of seascape on its grandest scale, however, is free to those who decide instead to take the much narrower, wandering old coast road which, climbing and plunging by turns, offers on clear days wondrous views far across the wide Firth of Clyde to Turnberry Bay on the Ayrshire coast.

From the last height before coming down to sea level again, the village of Southend is seen lying along its sandy shore, with Dunaverty Point rising majestically between broad curving beaches of gold, and the hills of Antrim showing blue across seventeen or so miles of ocean.

Very little remains today of the ancient stronghold of the MacDonald Lords of the Isles, which once topped Dunaverty Rock. Here, in his least fortunate days, Robert Bruce found sanctuary for a time; here much later James IV found his efforts to assume full kingship set at naught by the same still powerful clan; and here, in 1647, the last of that long line of Somerled fought his final battle. Far from those stirring times, Southend is today a sleepy golf and beach resort with an all-the-year-round population of something like half a hundred, where a century ago four times that number dwelt under much less favourable housing conditions.

Beyond Dunaverty Bay, on the way to Carskey—where are to be found perhaps the finest, most golden sands of all—the ruin of the ancient church of Kilcolmkill nestles beneath the high bluff of Keil Point. Close by, an older smaller cell is believed to be that founded by Columba, to whom the later building was dedicated. On a flat rocky surface, two foot-imprints are still believed by many to mark the spot where the saint first stepped ashore in Scotland. Most scholars are seemingly agreed that at least one footprint, that nearer the sea, is of sufficient antiquity to be likely to have had some connection with the ceremony of assuming kingship. There is moreover no reason to discredit the belief that the founder of Iona did visit this spot, if not on his first arrival in Scotland, then at least on a visit to his long-time friend and mentor, Ciaran, best loved and longest remembered of all the early missionaries to Kintyre, who gave his name to the loch on which the main town stands, and even to the town itself, centuries before a Campbell earl ever got a footing in the place.

Out to sea, the Isle of Sanda has yet another of the very large number of ruined chapels in the vicinity, this one dedicated to St Ninian.

Near Southend, on the shore, the burnt-out ruins of the original Keil School have the appearance of never having been looked on since that day in 1924 when the boys got their possessions out before the blazing roof fell in. Fluted columns and graceful arches stand amid the rubble, and soft-eyed cows graze in lush grass where once the rugby field and cricket ground resounded to the voices of boys long scattered the world over.

Soon the narrow road begins to climb steeply, with almost tropical vegetation on either side. A sudden corkscrew rise to 700ft leaves the fertile garden of Kintyre behind and presents a barren windswept waste of hills where only the toughest of heather can cling to rocks lashed by gales the year round.

Up and up goes the narrow ribbon, to 1,000ft, with glimpses of sea almost painfully blue to the far distant coast of Wigtownshire and, nearer, breaking lazily on fangs of black, age-old rock, with toy-like ships trailing white wakes.

At 1,350ft a narrow pass, known as The Gap, is reached; beyond this no vehicles are permitted except on lighthouse business. The lighthouse far below resembles, within the vast panorama, a toy some child has left on the edge of the sheerly vertical 300ft cliff. The coast of Ireland is only a dozen miles away, with houses, fields and trees standing out clearly. The lighthouse on Rathlin Island seems almost nearer than the one on the edge of the dizzy precipice below. From The Gap the narrow track plunges nearly 1,000ft in three-quarters of a mile, with fearsome hairpin bends. It is a very long way down to the peninsula's final milestone on the uttermost edge of the cliff, which states: 'Campbeltown 16 miles 1030 yds.'

The lighthouse is open to visitors from after 1 pm to an hour before sunset, at the discretion of the principal keeper. It was built by the Stevensons in 1820, though from 1788 a light of sorts had been maintained on this most fearsome of all headlands. The present beam is visible for 24 miles.

On the return journey, it is unnecessary to go back into Southend village before taking the faster inland route towards Campbeltown. Where the B842 road joins the north-west-bound A83, the way to Machrihanish turns off sharply to the left, skirting the Laggan, that vast one-time peat moss, running to immense sand dunes on the western shore. Over the years this moss has been largely reclaimed for agriculture, and now accommodates the RAF base and the civil airport. Above the dunes stretches the world-famed golf course.

Machrihanish village is nowadays quietly residential, with good hotel accommodation for golfers, but simply crying out for even one café to replace the tea-room which, once beloved of day trippers, is now the village hall. The village was once known as 'The Pans', from the days up to the eighteenth century when salt was produced here by the evaporation of sea water, and stands not far from the site of Kintyre's one and only coal mine which closed down in 1967. The future of Machrihanish probably lies in its broad beach of firm silvery sand that curves for nearly six miles to Westport, at the point where the main north-bound road out of Campbeltown, having skirted the Laggan, turns to follow the coast towards Tarbert.

Here is probably the most popular of all Kintyre's picnic spots, and the beginning—or the end, depending on how you look at it—of the biggest sand beach of Argyll's mainland. Here, mountainous wind-blown sand dunes provide deep sun-traps where an army might lie concealed; here, between the shore and the waving machair grasses crowning the dunes, conversation has to be shouted above the roar and crash of the enormous rollers which, even on days of complete air stillness, come marching in from the world's end—for there is no land westward of here nearer than Newfoundland across the empty Atlantic. Among the flotsam which dries out on this beauty spot, the attention of the writer was recently attracted by a notice board from a church in Boston, Massachusetts, informing him of the hours of service and Sunday school!

THE WEST SIDE

North-bound from Westport, it is about three miles along the picturesquely rock-strewn shore, with the good broad road ever winding and twisting, to the very charming old village of Bellochantuy, which is fronted by yet another long silver strand and enjoys the distinction of having the most frequently mispronounced place name in Kintyre. The original Gaelic *Bealach an t-sith*—The Fairies' Pass—should be pronounced something like 'Balloch-an-tshee'. Surely such a spelling— which is no more incorrect than that displayed on the signposts and ordnance survey maps—might in these days of tourism be brought into use, if only to prevent such a beautiful little place becoming immortalised as 'Bello Chanty'. No blame need be laid on visitors who, far from trying to be funny, are more often laughed at than with, over their efforts to enunciate Gaelic place names, without any help whatsoever from the map-makers or the Scottish Tourist Board.

This is the point on the road which gives the best view of the softly rounded green hills of Islay rising out of the sea. Lovely at any time of the day and in any weather, at sunset on a summer evening with the very slightest haze lingering in the west, the seaward prospect from the road just above Bellochantuy might defy adequate description even by a poet.

By little scalloped bays, the good broad road runs to Glen Barr, another pleasant village set on a steep hill over which the way drops to sea level again, towards Muasdale. By now the rugged hills of Jura are seen closely, reaching into the western sky, with Gigha lying closer inshore, tailed by the coffin-shaped Isle of Cara. It becomes plain to see why the plundering Norse rovers so coveted Kintyre, for, all the way up this west side, the agricultural land is as rich as any in Scotland, well farmed with mixed crops and grazing large herds of sleek-hided dairy cattle.

Just before Tayinloan, whence the ferry crosses to Gigha, yet one more ancient chapel, that of Killean, stands just to the left of the road. This is a beautifully preserved building, of late Norman architecture. In the east gable, two rounded windows with decorative work above have been built up. In the Largie vault, about ten of the best of the sculptured stones have been collected for protection from the weather. These are regarded by some authorities as amongst the finest stone carvings even in the West Highlands.

It is a fast road now, through the well-wooded, rhododendron-thicketed glen of Ronachan, where the road climbs briefly before losing sight of the western sea. Just at this point a close inshore reef has, over the centuries, become the meeting place for hundreds of grey Atlantic seals which enjoy the fishing of these sparkling waters. Especially on warm sunny days, these delightfully friendly creatures flipper their way on to the tops of the big flat rocks in large numbers; so popular have they become with passers-by that the authorities have recently found it necessary to construct a large parking area for the use of seal viewers. Beyond Ronachan, the way drops gently downward to the very delightful old village of Clachan, happily bypassed by the now fast road swooping upward to the very roof of the peninsula. Such bypasses, clearly the order of the Kintyre of today, bring carless peace to such villages as Clachan, where it is possible to wander without risk across the road to examine, say, the very interesting old church and churchyard.

From the high summit of the bypass, on the journey northward, the prospect is almost boundless and surely among the finest anywhere in the county, reaching, as it does, over the West Loch, beyond Kilberry and Knapdale into the blue distant hills of Mid Argyll.

From the height of Dun Skeig—overhanging the very narrow side road that wanders down by the West Loch and round by the hidden Loup into Clachan village again—the view is even more breathtaking, embracing the nearer isles and a much wider panorama of sea-cleft Argyll. Here, too, stands the second of Kintyre's two vitrified forts and, shining far below on the other side of the main road, the silvery sheet of Lochan Dughaill, where drainage in the last century brought to light the remains of two *crannogs*—lake dwellings of the Dark Ages.

Once more the road dips, to bring into sight the charming bypassed village of Whitehouse. This village in particular gives the impression of not having changed a great deal since four-in-hand coaches wound their way along the curving sickle of roadway scorned by the fast traffic of today; here the passing centuries have served only to mellow the stonework of the graceful old buildings.

Only a very little way onward lies the road junction to Skipness or northward into Tarbert, with all of Argyll beyond. Whichever road he chooses, the visitor will have seen much of Kintyre, and will know that there is much yet to see—another day.

10 TRADITIONAL SPEECH

W HEN, in Valparaiso or Bombay or any port between, a ship's captain is overheard to announce his intention of casting off 'the ee noo', it will be known that the speaker is a native of South Kintyre and that the business of casting off is to be put in hand immediately—not presently or in a few minutes, as might be implied by the English use of 'now'. The American 'right now' is perhaps the closest translation, though it fails to convey the exact moment of time implicit in 'the ee noo'—a phrase which the writer cannot trace as in use by any other than natives of the peninsula.

Much of the distinctive dialect, especially of South Kintyre, is still that brand of English called Lowland Scots, imported, along with those whose speech this was, from Ayrshire and the Clyde coast. The intonation, however, is peculiar to Kintyre itself, as is also the idiom in several cases, the latter bearing still the fading stamp of the ancient Gaelic tongue.

There is no native Gaelic in Kintyre today, save in the offshore Isle of Gigha. Both Campbeltown and Carradale support choirs which have distinguished themselves at the National Gaelic Mod, but any members of such choirs who still speak Gaelic are either incomers from the isles, or those who have acquired the language by study. This was far from being the state of affairs as recently as the early seventeenth century, when Gaelic was the only tongue of the native people—the descendants of those first Scots who founded the kingdom of Dalriada around the year 503.

From about 1640, the dialect of Kintyre, especially of the more populated southern areas, was profoundly affected by events which caused it to develop as a form of speech peculiarly recognisable wherever it is heard. Those events were, chiefly, the Colkitto Raids and the subsequent disturbances, which left many desolate acres; the plague, which wiped out more of the natives; and the plan, already being put in hand by the Marquis of Argyll to clear out as many as possible of the untrustworthy natives and replace them with settlers invited to come in from Ayrshire and Renfrewshire.

Wars and plague between them saw to it that little if any actual clearance was to prove necessary; but the plantation went ahead and the lowland settlement of Kintyre was carried out over the following hundred years. The newcomers used what was in those days the speech common to Lowland Scotland, not the dialect found in the same areas today, but a brand of early English which had only comparatively recently displaced the Gaelic tongue, the latter being, even then, still the speech in common use in isolated southern Ayrshire and in Galloway.

The settlers appear to have adopted a very strict policy of non-integration. It is highly probable that they believed the native Gaelic-speaking people to be little better than barbarians with whom they, as a superior race, could have nothing in common. They built their own church, the Lowland Church of Campbeltown, in 1654. There they worshipped their Lowland God in the only tongue they felt would be acceptable to Him; and when they died they were buried apart, in ground undefiled by Gaelic bones. Most especially were they determined that their children should grow up to speak with their own superior tongue. The success of these efforts was furthered by sending the children to school in Campbeltown, to a grammar school which, according to the Southend Parish Records, was established there as early as 1656.

There can be no doubt that the shrewd marquis and his

successors fostered and encouraged this state of separation of the Highlanders and Lowlanders. Fear of a rising in favour of the ousted MacDonalds took a long time to die; Argyll's overlordship of Kintyre would never be secure until he had disposed of the best and most fertile lands to hand-picked Presbyterian lairds and their dependants who, as has been seen, kept themselves very much to themselves, all the while being regarded by the native Highlanders with contempt.

In his *Book of Blaan*, the late Rev Angus MacVicar—who, in 1957, retired from fifty years of active ministry in the Parish of Southend—gives simple words to the natural outcome of a situation which must, after a time, have become something of an embarrassment to both sides.

> This state of affairs continued for well over a hundred years, probably to the beginning of the 19th century. This exclusiveness, I am led to believe, was more strictly observed on the part of the Lowlanders. But it broke down when their sons fell in love with the daughters of Highlanders and married them. And of course, vice versa. This brought them to a better understanding, and to have more respect for one another. Intermarriage, since then, has been so common that the two classes of the population can scarcely be distinguished from each other.

The above was written in 1967. Today there is no evidence that there ever were 'two classes'. From the middle of the nineteenth century the use of the Gaelic tongue, even in the playground, was actively discouraged by the schoolmasters; ridiculous, though not so very exaggerated tales are recounted of pupils being punished on suspicion of 'laughing in Gaelic'. Inevitably, intermarriage demanded a common tongue for the home; as inevitably, this became the speech of the next generation, to be passed on, again, to their children.

In this amalgamation, Lowland Scots predominated, with a rare Gaelic inflexion, a few examples of the Gaelic idiom, and still an occasional word adopted straight from the dying native speech. This is what gives to the South Kintyre brand of

Lowland Scots the peculiarities of vocabulary, intonation and idiom which set it apart from any dialect used in even the most closely neighbouring areas of the Scottish mainland.

A few examples of dialect regarded as peculiar to Kintyre may be given here.

The interrogative 'what' is rendered as 'hoot'—for example, 'Hoot wis keepan ye in that shop?' There is a relic of Gaelic idiom hidden in this inquiry. Note *'What was* keeping you?' in place of just 'What kept you?' Since there is no simple present tense of the Gaelic verb, the Gaelic speaker cannot say 'I run'; he must say 'I *am* running'. The same usage holds for the past tense and also for the future. Hence, 'I was sayin' tae the minister' not 'I *said* to the minister'. And, 'They'll be holdin' a meeting tomorrow' instead of 'they *will* hold a meeting'.

Another survival, this time of Gaelic pronunciation, is perpetuated in the Kintyre way of turning the emphasised vowel sound 'i' as in minister into 'ee' as in keep, making for such pronunciation as 'meenister', 'ceevil', 'conteenued', 'releegious' and so on. Note that in the first two examples, where 'minister' and 'civil' each have two short 'i' sounds, only the first syllable is given the 'ee' sound. This is always so, with the emphasis on the 'ee' sound, holding true to its Gaelic origin.

The clipped English vowel 'i' is, on the other hand, rendered as 'u'—trip becoming 'trup', and 'grip' and 'trim' becoming 'grup' and 'trum'. This is one more example of what might be called a fall-out from the original Gaelic of Kintyre.

Words in daily use which are almost purely Gaelic or a debased form of that tongue are very much less frequently heard since World War II, and are undoubtedly falling into complete disuse. When, in 1926, MacInnes collected material from the Kintyre dialect on behalf of the Scottish National Dialect Dictionary, he was able to list no fewer than 169 words of recognisable Gaelic origin, more than half of which he stated to be then in daily use, the others only occasionally heard.

163

Forty-five years later, only 7 per cent of the Gaelic words then noted survive in the dialect, and then mostly among older people, especially those connected with the fishing industry. Television and travel have largely contributed to a certain levelling process in the several dialects of southern Scotland, so that while, in the examples given below, an effort will be made to find usages peculiar to Kintyre, it must be understood that some forms may be recognisable as the speech of much of southern and mid-Scotland also.

Consonant terminals are in some cases dropped, in others altered and emphasised. For example 't' is always silent following on a 'k' sound, as in the following: 'He had great respec' for the exac' law, and was always stric' aboot the fac's o' the case.'

After 'n' the 'd' is silent. The statement, 'My friend didn't wish to spend money on a load of sand' would thus become 'Ma freen didna want tae spen' money on a load o' saan'.'

The terminal 'g' in nouns which end in 'ing' is always dropped, turning 'herring' and 'beading' into 'herrin' and 'beadin'; but in verbs, the 'ing' ending changes to 'an'—for example, 'crying' becomes 'cryan', 'waiting' 'waitan', and so on. Also it is noteworthy that where, in most Lowland Scots dialects, a child is referred to as a 'wean' (pronounced wane), in Kintyre the same child becomes a 'way-an', with two clear syllables.

Often a terminal 't' is added to such words as 'once' 'twice' and 'sudden'. Hence, 'A kent at wanct that if an attack came twicet in the same day, the end wad be suddent'.

In some words also, the terminal 'v' sound as in 'leave' is omitted: 'A wantit tae lea' her hame before twel' o' the clock'. In passing it may be noted that, in Kintyre, a young man does not *see* a girl home, he *leaves* her home.

Vowel changes are, in many cases, the same as those used in Lowland Scots wherever it is spoken; yet always with an inimitable inflexion peculiar to Kintyre. One example of this is the rendering of the short double vowel sound 'ea' as in 'peat' into the narrow 'a' as in 'hate'. Thus, the following exaggerated illustration might quite easily be overheard: 'A'm fair *bate* tae dress *nate* and *dacent*, withoot showin' *concate*, in times when guid claes is no *chape*'.

For some reason the same narrow but slightly longer 'a' as in 'blaze' makes the spoken word 'bleeze', while a mare is never anything but a 'meer', nor is a neighbour referred to other than as a 'neebour'. The changing of the short, broader 'a' means that 'after' is always 'efter', the family is the 'femily', a glass becomes a 'gless', a farm a 'ferm' and so on. The broad, longer 'a' sound, as in English 'ball', is rendered more like the single broad 'a' in 'bar', eg, 'waar' for war, 'scaar' for scare, 'whaar' for where, 'baal' for ball.

There are many idioms and turns of phrase which instantly identify the speaker with Kintyre. The use of the word 'although' to end a statement, here takes the place of the more commonly heard 'but' of the Clyde industrial area: 'She's fair improved at the dancin' although' and 'It's fine weather, but too dry although'.

The use of 'besides' in place of 'instead of' is another form not commonly heard out of Kintyre: 'It's fine the mail comin' in early, besides the wey it used tae be' or, 'It's grand havin' yer ain car, besides dependin' on lifts'.

Nothing is ever 'past' or 'beyond'. 'By' is the word used: 'The house is a full mile by the pier'; 'I thought he would stop, but he went right on by'; 'When the chair broke, she fair went by hersel' ' (with rage); 'They're sayin' the new man's a by-ordnar preacher' (beyond the ordinary).

'Chief' means particularly friendly, or close: 'Her and the wife up at the big hoose is aaful chief this while'. In the same way the word 'great' is used: 'Jock's wife's aaful great wi' big Jean the noo.'

'The noo'—for 'just now'—as used here means 'of recent times' and should not be confused with 'the ee noo' mentioned already as denoting a precise moment: 'If ye don't want tae miss the show, ye better set off the ee noo.'

The use of 'in it' to indicate existence is pure Gaelic idiom: 'Take care o' that book, it's the only copy that's in it'; 'It'll depend what weather's in it at the time'; 'There was no bread in it, the time o' the strike.'

To denote an unusual or extraordinary state of affairs, the employment of the word 'wild', sometimes spoken as 'wile', has become known as so typically Kintyre as to give rise to such jocular imitations as 'It's a wild calm night' or 'Them foxes are wild and tame!' Certainly it is quite usual to be told, 'It's wild the fish that's in it this year' or, 'He was usin' wild big stones for the road'.

'As' is frequently used in place of 'than': 'There's times when wood does better as stone'; 'Take a look at that bird—your eyes is better as mine'.

The Gaelic influence is once again shown to be strong where the preposition 'on' is used with a personal pronoun: 'She just lifted the cup when the handle broke on her'; 'His best cow went and died on him'; 'You better hide that ring or you'll get it stolen on you'.

'So bein' as' takes the place of 'if'—but only when the events spoken of are still in the future. For instance, one might say, in the past tense, 'If he was there, I didn't see him' or, in the present, 'Go to the show, if you like'. But, in the future, 'We'll be at the show the morn, so bein' as it stays dry'; 'A'll get a hair-cut on Monday, so bein' as Dan's no' too busy'.

In the personal pronoun, the accusative case is more commonly employed than the nominative, as, 'Her and him jist chanced tae meet at the pier'; 'Them that taalks most does the least work'.

A person is seldom spoken of as still living, but as 'still to the fore': 'A'm hearin' thon ould meenister's still tae the fore'. Note, incidentally, 'I'm hearing', instead of 'I hear', a clear relic of Gaelic idiom.

'I was about to say' is rendered in Kintyre as 'A was jist gaun *away* tae say'. Similarly the phrase 'took and' frequently occurs redundantly, as when a person says, 'A got a bucket o' herrin' this mornin' an' A took an' salted them right away' or, 'The rain went off, so A took an planted the bushes'.

While there are dozens of such examples of the Lowland Scots dialect, those selected are, in as many cases as possible, peculiar to Kintyre, especially the south of the peninsula, where usage of the dialect persists. At the same time it must be clearly understood that, though even among many of the younger people the forms quoted are still the speech of home, street, playground and shop, standard English of a very high quality comes readily into use when the occasion for it arises. The rate at which characteristic and often picturesque words and phrases have fallen into disuse since MacInnes presented his paper in 1926 points to a day when the dialect as once spoken in Kintyre will fall completely out of use, and be of interest to scholars only.

As witness to this decline in the everyday use of dialect, the following song, or ballad, once a favourite at rural concerts, was repeated to the writer many times during World War II by natives of Kintyre who could not, themselves, understand every word of it. It was written, in the last century, by John Brollachan—later Brodie—a Campbeltown native who became a minister of the Free Church, and it is probable that, in this song and others, he deliberately set out to employ words and phrases that were, even then, falling out of use in the everyday conversation of the people.

FLORY LOYNACHAN

O, it buite be an ogly thing
That mougres thus o'er me,
For I scrabbed at mysel' yestreen,
And could not bab an e'e.
My heart is all to muilins minsh'd,
Brye, smuirach, daps, and gum,
I'm a poor cruichach, spalyin' scrae,
My horts have strok me dumb.

Dear Flory Loynachan, if thou
Through Sanna's soun' wert toss't
And rouchled like a shougie-shoo
In a veshal with one most,
Though the night were makin' for a roil,
Though rallaich were the sea,
Though scorlins warpled my thowl pins,
My shallop would reach thee.

Thou'rt not a hochlan scleurach, dear,
As many trooshlach be;
Nor I a claty skybal, thus
To sclaffer after thee.
Yet haing the meishachan, where first
I felt love's maiglan smert,
And haing the boosach dyvour, too,
Who spoong'd from me thine heart.

O! rhane a yolus cronie—quick—
Across this rumpled brain!
Bring hickery-pickery, bring wallink,
Droshachs to soothe my pain!
Fire water, fire a spoucher full,
These frythan stouns to stay!
For like a sporrow's scaldachan
I'm gosping night and day!

Were I the laird of Achnaglach,
Or Kilmanshenachan fair,
Crockstaplemore, Kilwheepnach,
Feochag or Ballochgair;
Did I inherit Tayinroech,
Drumgarve or Ballochantee,
Creishlach or Coeran—daing the bit,
I'd fauchat them a' for thee!

O, the clabbydhu it loves the Trench,
The crouban, the quay-neb.
While the anachan and brollochan
They love the mussel-ebb;

The muirachbaan the Dorlin loves,
And the gleshan and guildee
They love to plouder through the loch,
But, Flory, I love thee.

A very necessary glossary for the above is best given verse by verse, rather than alphabetically.

1 Buite be: *Must be*
 Ogly: *Uncanny*
 Mougres: *Creeps over*
 Bab an e'e: *Shut an eye*
 To muilins minsh'd: *Crushed to crumbs*
 Brye, smuirach, daps and gum: *Powdered sandstone, very small coal, tiny flounders, and coal dust*
 Cruichach spalyin scrae: *Twisted splay-footed skinny creature*
2 Sanna's soun': *Sound, or strait of Sanda Isle*
 Rouchled: *Shaken*
 Shougie-shoo: *A rocking chair*
 Roil: *A hard blow*
 Rallaich: *Very stormy*
 Scorlins warpled my thowl pins: *Stringy seaweed strangled my rowlocks*
3 Hochlan: *Slovenly dressed*
 Scleurach; Gaelic, *sgliurach* a young seagull: inclined to *screech noisily*
 Trooshlach: *Common trash*
 Claty skybal: *An unwashed, idle youth*
 Sclaffer: *Walk drag-footed*
 Haing the meishachan: *Curse the social gathering*
 Maiglan: *Wounding*
 Boosach dyvour: *A sullen-mouthed, uncomely person*
4 Rhane a yolus cronie: *Sing a wise spell, or charm*
 Hickery-pickery, wallink, droshachs: *A magic draught compounded of bitter aloes and drugs extracted from herbs*
 Spoucher: *A wooden ladle used for baling boats*
 Frythan stouns: *Burning pains, as of frying*
 A sporrow's scaldachan: *An unfledged, featherless sparrow*
5 Daing the bit: *Devil the thought*
 Fauchat: *Reject absolutely*
6 Clabbydhu: *The large mussel*

The Trench: *Trench Point, entrance to Campbeltown Loch*
Crouban: *Crab*
Quay-neb: *The nose or end of the quay*
Anachan, Brollochan: *Common mud-loving bi-valves*
Muirachbaan: *A white shell fish*
Dorlin: *A scythe of shingle left dry at ebb*
Gleshan and Guildee: *Fish of the saithe and cod family*

A number of the words noted above are either debased Gaelic or have Gaelic roots. Many more, however, belong to that version of Lowland Scots which was, in fact, ancient English, and which was brought into Kintyre by the settlers from Ayrshire and Renfrewshire.

(For the written version of 'Flory Loynachan', the writer is indebted to the late Rev Angus J. MacVicar. Spelling in a few cases might differ from other written versions.)

11   THE CHANGING SCENE

FOR the third or perhaps even the fourth time in its long history, Kintyre is taking a confident step into the future.

First came the earliest men, who dwelt in caves and rude huts, and clung to the shores where it was easier to feed their families, clearing very little of the good land for crop cultivation.

Next came the highly civilised Scots to found the first kingdom which was, in time, to become the Lordship of the Isles, in the hands of Clan Donald. This was followed, in times comparatively recent, by the revolution which brought about the Campbell overlordship of Kintyre, with its resultant period of resettlement and recolonisation, the gradual fusion of the two peoples into one, a sound agricultural policy and, for the first time since history began, an end to internal wars.

Now the fourth and most confident forward step in Kintyre's social and economic life has been taken. Like the Lords of the Isles before them, though pressed not by the edge of the sword as much as by the hard cold wood of unlined coffers, the house of Argyll has given up its hold on the peninsula, which succeeding members of its family had done so much, in their several days, to weld into the live, forward-striving community settled there by the mid-twentieth century.

RURAL LIFE

The disposal by sale of the vast Argyll estates in Kintyre has resulted in the majority of the former tenant farmers becoming their own landlords—lairds in their own right. Their original purchase has, naturally, increased greatly in value since 1955, contributing in no small measure to the undoubted air of prosperity which is abroad in Kintyre today.

Nor have the proprietor farmers alone benefited from the general upsurge in agriculture. Those who work the land for a wage are much better housed, much better paid. Gone are the days of the 'feeing market', when, even as lately as between the two major wars, shepherds, ploughmen and cattlemen paraded themselves in town every six months, open to the offer of a change from any farmer seeking a likely helper. There, verbal agreements were entered into; a ploughman moving, with his 'cist', as his large trunk was always called, from farm to farm, each six months, if the fancy took him. Gone with this system are the days of the farm 'bothy', often a barely furnished room above the stable, where the single farm hands at the end of a very long day's work—hours were seldom specified—stamped their feet to the music of a melodeon or a fiddle, which one or another of them seemed always able to acquire out of his meagre wage, always paid six-monthly; by which time, in very many cases, most of the sum was already pledged.

In the case of the married farm worker, a change simply meant the transference by cart of his household gear from one farm cottage to another, perhaps miles away. This move was always called a 'flitting', though the slow ponderous march of the great Clydesdale horse drawing the cart surely had little to do with the commonly understood meaning of the verb 'to flit'! At all events, the farm worker and his equally hard-working wife could always know that, when they finally arrived, their furniture was going to fit in without difficulty—since one farm cottage differed very little from another.

There is a great deal of nostalgia, and not entirely without reason, for those not so long gone days. Within the family, ties were closer; because there was nowhere to go, sons and daughters stayed home in the evening time and neighbours might call round, one good at story-telling, another carrying a fiddle or melodeon. That was in winter only, of course. In hay or harvest times of the year, long working hours saw to it that even a walk in the scented dusk with the very attractive kitchen lass from the next farm had to be a rare pleasure, especially as she also might well have been tying corn sheaves by hand in all the heat of the long day.

A dance in the village school or in a barn was something to be looked forward to for many weeks and engaged in with the kind of vigour that demanded a high degree of physical fitness; and it would be talked of for as many weeks afterwards. The music for such events was supplied by an easily recruited band of local musicians who would have laughed in disbelief at the thought of anyone ever being paid for such a service. They simply took off their jackets and blew, or scraped or squeezed, according to instrument; and might be encouraged to renewed efforts by the simple dispensation of the contents of a Campbeltown bottle, at suitable intervals.

Gone is the 'feeing' market, gone the farm 'bothy', the traditional 'flitting' from one low-roofed farm cottage to another. The ploughman homeward plods his weary way no more. More often than not he travels between farm and neat modern home in his own car; and he is far from weary, since his comparatively short working day has been passed driving some piece of agricultural machinery.

It is to be supposed that this is how things ought to be. Yet the nostalgia lingers among the older people, who see changes not always entirely satisfying. First there is a different relationship within the family, a severing of those close ties that once made the low-raftered cottage with its floored loft a warm place long before electric heating was invented. Families are smaller, for one thing—and just as well, or they would need more cars. It is common enough for the son of the house to drive into town several evenings of the week to foregather with his friends; at the same time his sister is whisked off in her boy friend's fast car, perhaps forty miles northward to Lochgilphead, to attend a dance where the musicians will receive something like £50–£75 for their night's work. Neighbours do not just drop in, as they used to; they are watching television.

Now, this is far from being a gloomy picture of life in Kintyre. It represents a people living as they choose, in a freedom dearly bought. And this freedom of choice is emphasised by the still widening range of spare-time activities open to both young and old in every village and rural community in the peninsula.

The advance of tourism encourages the revival of ancient crafts. There are still local dances, evening classes in a wide variety of subjects, whist drives, excellent dramatic societies and bridge clubs. There is the Women's Rural Institute, and there is the excellent mobile county library which, astonishingly in these days, dispenses an average of two thousand books per week.

POLITICS AND LOCAL GOVERNMENT

The people of Kintyre share one member of parliament with their island and mainland neighbours of the county, and tend not to trouble him with matters they are perfectly capable of dealing with in their own way. None of the new younger voters remember the day when anyone other than a Conservative and Unionist represented the county at Westminster. In recent years, however, since so many more people are now their own lairds and no longer feel obliged to vote with the landlord who was good enough to provide a comfortable carriage to take them to the polling station, there has been a noticeable swing to nationalism.

Into local government, in which there is an equal amount of interest, politics does not enter at all. This is in the hands of the county council, with a full time county clerk and a full time district clerk for districts the size of Kintyre, Mid Argyll, Lorn. Members of the council are amateurs of any profession and their political views are their own affair.

However, this happy position may well be changed when, for all administrative purposes, Kintyre, along with the rest of Argyll, is absorbed as part of a large slice of south-west Scotland into a rearranged local government area.

THE VIEW AHEAD

Kintyre has been, almost overnight, projected into the late twentieth century, and that by the combined effort, with native tenacity of purpose, of the people themselves.

There is yet much to be achieved. While unemployment is relatively low in the rural areas, the industrial burgh of Campbeltown has so often suffered in this respect that much effort is yet needed before a safe state of prosperity can reign there.

Job prospects

The hard core of unemployment in the town exists at the time of writing as a total of 274, of which only 51 are women; 54 men and 66 women have part-time work only, while 90 married women seek jobs—a grand total of 484 people unemployed. In addition, 29 girls and 50 boys leave school at the age of 16 each year, while 8 boys and 5 girls annually leave between that age and the completion of the full course—a disturbing total of 92.

At present, only a handful of these youngsters can find employment in the town. Most, especially the girls, will have to leave the peninsula altogether, seeking training as nurses, hairdressers, etc. Naturally, also, both girls and boys who complete the school course and go on to university or other training are at present mostly lost to their native area forever. The situation with these last must always remain the same; perhaps it is not a bad thing that Kintyre is thus able to confer on the rest of the world the benefits of this 'brain drain'.

For the adult unemployed, and for early school-leavers, the determined efforts of the town council in conjunction with the

Highlands and Islands Development Board are at present containing the position. New industries are being sought with every day that passes. Among those attracted to Campbeltown in recent times are a factory for servicing aircraft components, a ball-point-ink manufacturing firm, and a comprehensive bakery—the latter an extension of a long-established 'native' firm, McIlchere & Son. If there is a solution to the unemployment problem which determined search will bring to light, then it will be found.

The problem at Tarbert, Kintyre's only other centre of population, is less acute. Here, the once busy boat-building yard which failed a few years back is again providing work, and there are the sailmaker's loft, the sea-food factory and the busy tweed mill, the two latter being industries of fairly recent establishment.

Tourism

From all the signs, the scarcely exploited industry of tourism could bring to Kintyre a new and exciting prosperity. The region has all the attractions of European holiday areas, as well as some not to be found anywhere else. Up till now, the surface of this growing industry has scarcely been scratched—and this is in the view of the Area Tourist Officer, whose appointment to a full-time post indicates the potential value of the industry.

At present, over the length and width of Kintyre, good hotels provide a total of 350 bedrooms, while 340 more are available in private homes registered with the organisation. Self-catering cottages, an increasingly popular form of holiday accommodation, are on offer to the number of 55. Touring caravan stances, as modernly equipped as any in Europe, number 175, while there are 60 static caravans for rent, sited in surroundings of incomparable beauty, close to beaches, golf or fishing.

This is an industry which will undoubtedly expand in the years ahead. With the upsurge of interest in such activities as archaeology, sea-angling and pony trekking the revenue from tourism could double within the present decade.

Yet still Kintyre remains and will remain unspoilt. To some it may seem a pity that, in the making of the fine fast highways, so many picturesque little villages have had to be bypassed, but those who have their homes there have no doubts on the matter. Some who are old enough remember the original roads, often steep, with winding ways well suited to allowing a tired horse a moment's respite from pressure on the collar. Those were the roads which grew, a little at a time, out of the need for men to get between farm and farm along both coasts. On the east side, where in its single-track state much of the original road is still in use, many of the old stone bridges attract so much attention from delighted tourists that occasional small traffic jams result from the determination of such visitors to take photographs of something they are clearly afraid might not be there tomorrow.

Strangers will come, and build their houses and settle here; but strangers have come, and settled, and been received into the community since the Norse rovers first landed on the coasts, where it is probable that some of their descendants remain to this day.

Seven thousand years have passed since men first said, 'This is Kintyre. Let us make this our home.' In that time kings have come and gone. Chieftains and lords have risen and fallen. Kintyre of the windswept rocks, the crashing sunlit waves, the wide green spaces, the rolling moors and hills is still there, the head of the land.

One day the sun will shine warmly over quiet seas; the next, only the tough heather will cling to the hills, flattened by the might of screaming winds. Fair or foul, the descendants of those first men will smile, or shrug their shoulders, and say— without uttering the words—'This is Kintyre. This is our home.'

BIBLIOGRAPHY

BARBOUR, J. *The Bruce* (Alexander Maclehose & Co, 1934)

BEDE, CUTHBERT. 'Argyll Highlands', *Celtic Monthly* (1902)

———. *Glencreggan*, vols 1–2 (Longman, 1861)

BLUE, A. WYLIE. 'Campbeltown Yesterday', *Campbeltown Courier* (1942)

CAMPBELL, LORD ARCHIBALD. *Records of Argyll* (Blackwood, 1885)

CAMPBELL, MARION. *Mid Argyll, A Handbook of History* (Antiquarian Society of Mid Argyll, 1970)

CAMPBELL, MARY STREETE. 'A Nonagenarian's Memoirs' (reprint from *Campbeltown Courier* preserved in Campbeltown Free Library)

DARLING, FRASER. *West Highland Survey* (Oxford University Press, 1955)

DUNBAR, J. G. and DUNCAN, A. A. M. *Scottish Historical Review*, vol L, 1, no 149 (University of Glasgow, 1971)

FARR, A. D. *The Campbeltown & Machrihanish Light Railway* (Oakwood Press, 1969)

GRAHAM, ANGUS. 'Skipness' (MS preserved in Campbeltown Library)

GRANT, I. F. *The Lordship of the Isles* (Moray Press, 1935)

HMSO. *Census 1961 Scotland County Report*, vol 1, 7, *Argyll*

———. *Report of Highland Transport Board*, 1967

JOHNSTON, K. *Southend through the Ages* (Campbeltown, nd)

Kintyre Club. *Historical Sketches of the Peninsula* (Kintyre Club, 1884, preserved in the Campbeltown Free Library)

MacDONALD, C. M. *3rd Statistical Account* (*Argyll*) (Collins, 1961)

———. *History of Argyll* (Holmes, 1950)

MACECHERN, C. VICTOR A. *The Book of Old Castlehill* (Constable, 1921)

McINNES, L. *Dialect of South Kintyre* (*Campbeltown Courier*, 1934)

MacINTOSH, PETER. *History of Kintyre* (*Campbeltown Courier*, 1929)

MacKAY, FRANK FORBES. *MacNeil of Carskey* (McDonald, 1955)

MacKENZIE, A. *The Highland Clearances* (Alex Maclaren, 1883)

MacKERRAL, ANDREW. *Kintyre in the 17th Century* (Oliver & Boyd, 1948)

178

MacMILLAN, NIGEL. *The Campbeltown & Machrihanish Light Railway* (David & Charles, 1970)

MacTAGGART, COL CHARLES. *The Lowland Church of Campbeltown* (*Campbeltown Courier*, 1924)

——. *Some Relics of Old Kintyre* (*Campbeltown Courier*, 1925)

——. 'The Old Kilkerran Graveyard', 'Life in Campbeltown in the 18th Century', 'Provosts of Campbeltown', 'Kintyre in the 17th Century' (Papers read before the Kintyre Antiquarian Society, 1922–3, and preserved in Campbeltown Library)

MacVICAR, REV A. J. *The Book of Blaan* (*Oban Times*, 1965)

MacVICAR, ANGUS. *Lifeboat Green to White* (Brockhampton Press, 1965)

——. *Rescue Call* (Kaye & Ward, 1967)

O'DELL, A. C. and WALTON, K. *The Highlands and Islands of Scotland* (Nelson, 1962)

Royal Commission on the Ancient and Historical Monuments of Scotland. *Argyll*, vol 1 (1972)

Scottish Women's Rural Institute (Largieside). *A Short History of Largieside* (Largieside SWRI, 1966)

—— (Machrihanish). *Our Village History* (Machrihanish SWRI, 1966)

SMITH, JOHN D. *Smith's Argyll* (G. & W. Nicol, 1805)

SMITH, W. Jr. *Views of Campbeltown and Neighbourhood* (1835)

Statistical Account of Scotland, The, no xxx, 5 (William Creech, 1791)

Statistical Account of Scotland, The New (Blackwood, 1845)

THOMSON, REV D. P. *Kintyre Through the Ages* (The Church of Scotland Office, 1940)

——. *It Happened in Kintyre* (The Church of Scotland Office, 1949)

THOMSON, T. HARVEY. *The Ancient Churches and Chapels of Kintyre* (*Campbeltown Courier*, 1934)

University of Edinburgh. *Scottish Studies*, vol 14 (1970)

Various Contributors. *Campbeltown 1700–1950* (Campbeltown Week Publications Committee, 1950)

WHITE, CAPT T. P. *Archaeological Sketches in Scotland* (Blackwood, 1873)

It is only fair to advise readers that several items listed above will be difficult to obtain, especially the papers of Col MacTaggart and some of the reprints from the *Campbeltown Courier*, but they may be examined at leisure in Campbeltown Free Library.

ACKNOWLEDGEMENTS

For unstinting help in the preparation of this work, the author returns sincere thanks to Mr E. P. MacKiernan, Librarian at Campbeltown Free Library; Mr Anthony McGrory, ex-Lifeboat Secretary; Mr Lachlan MacKinnon, Area Tourist Officer; Mr Duncan Colville; James M. B. Wright Esq of Auchinellan; Elizabeth Lorimer and Mrs Joyce Campbell.

INDEX

Italic page numbers indicate illustrations.

INDEX

INDEX